The Rez Sisters

The Rez Sisters

a play in two acts by
Tomson Highway

FIFTH
HOUSE
PUBLISHERS

Published by
Fifth House Ltd.
A Fitzhenry & Whiteside Company
195 Allstate Parkway
Markham, ON L3R 4T8
www.fifthhousepublishers.ca

Songs: "Crazy," © 1961 Tree Publishing Co. Inc., c/o Dunbar Music. Reprinted by permission. All rights reserved. "Texas When I Die," © 1977 and 1978 Tree Publishing Co. Inc., c/o Dunbar Music. Reprinted by permission. All rights reserved. "I'm Thinking of You," Tomson Highway, CAPAC 1984.

Cover design and illustration by Dean Pickup, Dpict Visual Communications
Printed in Canada

34 33 32 20

Fifth House Ltd. gratefully acknowledges with thanks the Canada Council for the Arts, the Ontario Arts Council, and the Department of Canadian Heritage for their support. We acknowledge the financial support of the Government of Canada through the Canada Book Fund (CBF) for our publishing activities.

Library and Archives Canada Cataloguing in Publication
Highway, Tomson, 1951-
The rez sisters.
Play. ISBN 978-0-92007944-7
I. Title.
PS8565.I34R4 1988 C812'.54 C88-098133-4
PR9199.3.H53R4 1988

For my mother, Pelagie Philomene Highway, a Rez Sister from way back. Keetha kichi ooma masinay-igan, Mama.

Tomson Highway was born on his father's trap-line on a
remote island on Maria Lake away up in northern Manitoba,
where it meets the borders of Saskatchewan and the Northwest
Territories. Maria Lake is about 100 miles north of the reserve
Tomson belongs to - Brochet, Manitoba - which is located
76 miles, as the crow flies, northwest of the mining town of
Lynn Lake, Man., northern end of the CN rail line. He was
born in a tent, like all his brothers and sisters, in the middle
of a snowbank on December 6, 1951, not 10 feet from the
dog-sled in which they travelled in those days.

Tomson's father, Joe Highway, was originally from the Pelican
Narrows Indian Reserve in northeastern Saskatchewan and his
ancestors come from this "rez" and from Cumberland House,
Saskatchewan. Joe Highway was a trapper/fisherman and a
legendary dog-sled racer. He won the championship at the
World Dog Derby at The Pas Trappers' Festival in February
1951, nine months before Tomson was born. One of Tomson's
older brothers, Swanson Highway, won this same event twice,
February 1962 and February 1964. Several relatives have won
this race many times over the years.

Tomson is the 11th of 12 children, five boys and seven girls, of which only three of the former and three of the latter are alive today. For the first six years of his life he lived an exquisitely beautiful nomadic lifestyle among the lakes and forests of remote northwestern Manitoba, trapping in winter, fishing in summer. Cree was the only language spoken and to this day, the older brothers and sisters don't speak English, though they do speak Chipewyan as well as Cree. Tomson learned to speak English at six years and became comfortably fluent in the language only in his late teens.

Tomson was sent to a Roman Catholic boarding school at the Guy Hill Indian Residential School in The Pas, Manitoba, at the age of six. He stayed there until age 15, when he finished grade nine. During these years at school Tomson was able to visit home for only two months every summer. Then he was sent to Churchill High School in Winnipeg where he lived in a series of white foster homes. He graduated in June 1970.

After high school, Tomson spent two years at the University of Manitoba Faculty of Music studying piano, which he had picked up at the boarding school at the age of 13. Tomson then spent a year in London, England, studying to be a concert pianist under William Aide, later a renowned teacher at the University of Toronto's Faculty of Music. He then returned to the University of Manitoba for one year, followed by a move with his piano teacher and mentor to the University of Western Ontario in London, where he graduated with a Bachelor of Music Honors in May 1975. Tomson stayed an extra year to complete the English courses required for a Bachelor of Arts degree. This is where he met - and worked with - James Reaney, perhaps one of English Canada's most respected playwrights/poets. Tomson also saw his first Michel Tremblay play at this time.

Once out of university, Tomson went to work for seven years with Native organizations and Native people at The Native Peoples' Resource Centre (a cultural center) in London, Ontario, and The Ontario Federation of Indian Friendship Centres in Toronto. During these years he worked with cultural programs, Native inmates in correctional centers and prisons, children's recreational programs, and other Native enterprises. His work enabled him to travel extensively around Canada - within the province of Ontario in particular - while meeting and working with (and just plain falling in love with over and over again) Native people on reserves, in friendship centers, in prisons, on the streets, and in the bars ... just generally familiarizing himself intimately with the organizational network of Native lives and politics in this country.

Then he turned 30 and decided it was time to put all this "training" and preparation together. Tomson started writing plays. If he couldn't put Chopin and "the rez" together, then he would write plays about "the rez," just as Michel Tremblay wrote about "The Main."

His first plays were performed to mostly Native audiences on reserves and in urban community centers. In addition to his writing, Tomson has worked with other Native theater companies - notably in Sioux Lookout, Ontario, and West Bay, Manitoulin Island - in various capacities (actor, musical director, director), touring Indian reserves far and wide.

In December 1986 *The Rez Sisters* hit the mainstream, taking Tomson by surprise. The play won the Dora Mavor Moore Award for best new play in Toronto's 1986-87 theater season and was further honored as one of the runners-up - along with *Jessica* by Linda Griffiths - for the Floyd S. Chalmers Award for the outstanding Canadian play of 1986. *The Rez*

Sisters performed to sold-out audiences during a cross-Canada tour from October to February 1988 (cities included Ottawa, Winnipeg, Toronto, Regina, and Vancouver). In August 1988 *The Rez Sisters* was one of only two productions to represent Canada on the Mainstage of the Edinburgh International Festival.

The next Highway play is *Dry Lips Oughta Move to Kapuskasing*, which was recently workshopped at Playwrights' Workshop Montreal. The play will appear as part of Native Earth Performing Arts' 1988-89 season. *Dry Lips* is a commission from the Prairie Theatre Exchange in Winnipeg and is what Tomson calls the flip-side to *The Rez Sisters* - featuring seven Indian men and a female Nanabush. The game this time is hockey!

Tomson has just completed his second season as Artistic Director of Native Earth Performing Arts Inc., Toronto's only professional Native theater company and one of only a small handful of such organizations in North America. A large part of the company's mandate is the development of Native playwrights and the establishment of a Native dramatic literature.

Tomson Highway's ambition in life is to make "the rez" cool, to show and celebrate what funky folk Canada's Indian people really are.

Acknowledgements

The Rez Sisters was workshopped at the De-ba-jeh-mu-jig Theatre Company, West Bay, Manitoulin Island, Ontario, in February 1986 with Mary Assiniwe, Greta Cheechoo, Gloria Eshkibok, Mary Green and Doris Linklater under the direction of Larry Lewis.

The Rez Sisters was first produced by the Act IV Theatre Company and Native Earth Performing Arts Inc. at the Native Canadian Centre of Toronto, on November 26, 1986, with the following:

Directed by Larry Lewis
Lighting Design by Patsy Lang
Set & Costume Design by Marilyn Bercovich
Music by David Tomlinson

Pelajia Patchnose - Gloria Miguel
Philomena Moosetail - Muriel Miguel
Marie-Adele Starblanket - Monique Mojica
Annie Cook - Anne Anglin
Emily Dictionary - Gloria Eshkibok
Veronique St. Pierre - Margaret Cozry
Zhaboonigan Peterson - Sally Singal
Nanabush - Rene Highway
Bingo Girl - Cheryl Mills

Production Manager - Jennifer Stein
Stage Manager - Joseph Boccia
Assistant Stage Manager - Luanne Naponse

The author wishes to extend his deep gratitude to these and the following individuals: Cindy Ball, Micah Barnes, Bernard J. Bomers, Jean McNeil, Billy Merasty, Daniel David Moses, Barbara Nahwegahbow, Jesse Nishihata, Maxine Noel, Delia Opekokew, Carol Rowntree, Kaaydah B. Schatten, Eugene Stickland.

And a special thanks to Elaine Bomberry, Tracy Bomberry, Raymond Lalonde, and Larry Lewis.

Production Notes

The role of Nanabush in *The Rez Sisters* is to be played by a male dancer - modern, ballet, or traditional. Stage directions for this mostly silent Nanabush are indicated very sparingly in this script. Only his most "essential" appearances are explicitly set out.

The music for *The Rez Sisters*, in its first productions, was provided by a musician who played at least 30 different percussion instruments from drum kit to bells to rattles, etc. This is the way I find the "soundscape" and the rhythm of this piece to be most effectively underlined.

Both Cree and Ojibway are used freely in this text for the reasons that these two languages, belonging to the same linguistic family, are very similar and that the fictional reserve of Wasaychigan Hill has a mixture of both Cree and Ojibway residents.

A Note on Nanabush

The dream world of North American Indian mythology is inhabited by the most fantastic creatures, beings, and events. Foremost among these beings is the "Trickster," as pivotal and important a figure in the Native world as Christ is in the realm of Christian mythology. "Weesageechak" in Cree, "Nanabush" in Ojibway, "Raven" in others, "Coyote" in still others, this Trickster goes by many names and many guises. In fact, he can assume any guise he chooses. Essentially a comic, clownish sort of character, he teaches us about the nature and the meaning of existence on the planet Earth; he straddles the consciousness of man and that of God, the Great Spirit.

Some say that "Nanabush" left this continent when the whiteman came. We believe he is still here among us - albeit a little the worse for wear and tear - having assumed other guises. Without him - and without the spiritual health of this figure - the core of Indian culture would be gone forever.

Cast of Characters

Pelajia Patchnose, 53

Philomena Moosetail, 49, sister of Pelajia

Marie-Adele Starblanket, 39, half-sister of Pelajia & Philomena

Annie Cook, 36, sister of Marie-Adele & half-sister of the other two

Emily Dictionary, 32, sister of Annie & ditto

Veronique St. Pierre, 45, sister-in-law of all the above

Zhaboonigan Peterson, 24, mentally disabled adopted daughter of Veronique

Nanabush - who plays the Seagull (the dancer in white feathers), the Nighthawk (the dancer in dark feathers), and the Bingo Master.

Time: Late summer, 1986.
Place: The Wasaychigan Hill Indian Reserve, Manitoulin Island, Ontario. (Note: "Wasaychigan" means "window" in Ojibway.)

Act One

It is mid-morning of a beautiful late August day on the Wasaychigan Hill Indian Reserve, Manitoulin Island, Ontario. Pelajia Patchnose is alone on the roof of her house, nailing shingles on. She wears faded blue denim men's cover-alls and a baseball cap to shade her eyes from the sun. A brightly-colored square cushion belonging to her sister, Philomena Moosetail, rests on the roof beside her. The ladder to the roof is off-stage.

PELAJIA:

Philomena. I wanna go to Toronto.

PHILOMENA:

From offstage.

Oh, go on.

PELAJIA:

Sure as I'm sitting away up here on the roof of this old house. I kind of like it up here, though. From here, I can see half of Manitoulin Island on a clear day. I can see the chimneys, the tops of apple trees, the garbage heap behind Big Joey's dumpy little house. I can see the seagulls circling over Marie-Adele Starblanket's white picket fence. Boats on the North Channel I wish I was on, sailing away somewhere. The mill at Espanola, a hundred miles away ... and that's with just a bit of squinting. See? If I had binoculars, I could see the superstack in Sudbury. And if I were Superwoman, I could see the CN Tower in Toronto. Ah, but I'm just plain old Pelajia Rosella Patchnose and I'm here in plain, dusty, boring old Wasaychigan Hill ... Wasy ... waiting ... waiting ... nailing shining shingles with my trusty silver hammer on the roof of Pelajia Rosella Patchnose's little two-bedroom welfare house. Philomena. I wanna go to Toronto.

Philomena Moosetail comes up the ladder to the roof with one shingle and obviously hating it. She is very well-dressed, with a skirt, nylons, even heels, completely impractical for the roof.

PHILOMENA:

Oh, go on.

PELAJIA:

I'm tired, Philomena, tired of this place. There's days I wanna leave so bad.

PHILOMENA:

But you were born here. All your poop's on this reserve.

PELAJIA:

Oh, go on.

PHILOMENA:

You'll never leave.

PELAJIA:

Yes, I will. When I'm old.

PHILOMENA:

You're old right now.

PELAJIA:

I got a good 30 years to go . . .

PHILOMENA:

. . . and you're gonna live every one of them right here beside me . . .

PELAJIA:

. . . maybe 40 . . .

PHILOMENA:

. . . here in Wasy.

Tickles Pelajia on the breasts.

Chiga-chiga-chiga.

PELAJIA:

Yelps and slaps Philomena's hand away.

Oh, go on. It's not like it used to be.

PHILOMENA:

Oh, go on. People change, places change, time changes things. You expect to be young and gorgeous forever?

PELAJIA:

See? I told you I'm not old.

PHILOMENA:

Oh, go on. You.

PELAJIA:

"Oh, go on. You." You bug me like hell when you say that.

PHILOMENA:

You say it, too. And don't give me none of this "I don't like this place. I'm tired of it." This place is too much inside your blood. You can't get rid of it. And it can't get rid of you.

PELAJIA:

Four thirty this morning, I was woken by . . .

PHILOMENA:

Here we go again.

PELAJIA:

... Andrew Starblanket and his brother, Matthew. Drunk. Again. Or sounded like ...

PHILOMENA:

Nothing better to do.

PELAJIA:

... fighting over some girl. Heard what sounded like a baseball bat landing on somebody's back. My lawn looks like the shits this morning.

PHILOMENA:

Well, I like it here. Myself, I'm gonna go to every bingo and I'm gonna hit every jackpot between here and Espanola and I'm gonna buy me that toilet I'm dreaming about at night ... big and wide and very white ...

PELAJIA:

Aw-ni-gi-naw-ee-dick.[1]

PHILOMENA:

I'm good at bingo.

PELAJIA:

So what! And the old stories, the old language. Almost all gone ... was a time Nanabush and Windigo and everyone here could rattle away in Indian fast as Bingo Betty could lay her bingo chips down on a hot night.

---

1 Oh, go on. (Ojibway)

5

PHILOMENA:

Pelajia Rosella Patchnose. The sun's gonna drive you crazy.

And she descends the ladder.

PELAJIA:

Everyone here's crazy. No jobs. Nothing to do but drink and screw each other's wives and husbands and forget about our Nanabush.

From offstage Philomena screams. She fell down the ladder.

Philomena!

As she looks over the edge of the roof.

What are you doing down there?

PHILOMENA:

What do you think? I fell.

PELAJIA:

Bring me some of them nails while you're down there.

PHILOMENA:

Whining and still from offstage, from behind the house.

You think I can race up and down this ladder? You think I got wings?

PELAJIA:

You gotta wear pants when you're doing a man's job. See? You got your skirt ripped on a nail and now you can see your thighs. People gonna think you just came from Big Joey's house.

PHILOMENA:

She comes up the ladder in a state of disarray.

Let them think what they want. That old cow Gazelle Nataways ... always acting like she thinks she's still a spring chicken. She's got them legs of hers wrapped around Big Joey day and night ...

PELAJIA:

Philomena. Park your tongue. My old man has to go the hundred miles to Espanola just to get a job. My boys. Gone to Toronto. Only place educated Indian boys can find decent jobs these days. And here I sit all broken-hearted.

PHILOMENA:

Paid a dime and only farted.

PELAJIA:

Look at you. You got dirt all over your backside.

Turning her attention to the road in front of her house and standing up for the first and only time.

And dirt roads! Years now that old chief's been making speeches about getting paved roads "for my people" and still we got dirt roads all over.

PHILOMENA:

Oh, go on.

PELAJIA:

When I win me that jackpot next time we play bingo in Espanola ...

PHILOMENA:

Examining her torn skirt, her general state of disarray, and fretting over it.

Look at this! Will you look at this! Ohhh!

PELAJIA:

... I'm gonna put that old chief to shame and build me a nice paved road right here in front of my house. Jet black. Shiny. Make my lawn look real nice.

PHILOMENA:

My rib-cage!

PELAJIA:

And if that old chief don't wanna make paved roads for all my sisters around here ....

PHILOMENA:

There's something rattling around inside me!

PELAJIA:

... I'm packing my bags and moving to Toronto.

Sits down again.

PHILOMENA:

Oh, go on.

> *She spies Annie Cook's approach a distance up the hill.*

Why, I do believe that cloud of dust over there is Annie Cook racing down the hill, Pelajia.

PELAJIA:

Philomena. I wanna go to Toronto.

PHILOMENA:

She's walking mighty fast. Must be excited about something.

PELAJIA:

Never seen Annie Cook walk slow since the day she finally lost Eugene to Marie-Adele at the church 19 years ago. And even then she was walking a little too fast for a girl who was supposed to be broken-heart ... *Stopping just in time and laughing.* ... heart-broken.

> *Annie Cook pops up the top of the ladder to the roof.*

ANNIE:

> *All cheery and fast and perky.*

Halloooo! Whatchyou doing up here?

PELAJIA:

There's room for only so much weight up here before we go crashing into my kitchen, so what do you want?

ANNIE:

Just popped up to say hi.

PELAJIA:

And see what we're doing?

ANNIE:

Well ...

PELAJIA:

Couldn't you see what we're doing from up where you were?

ANNIE:

Confidentially, to Philomena.

Is it true Gazelle Nataways won the bingo last night?

PHILOMENA:

Annie Cook, first you say you're gonna come with me and then you don't even bother showing up. If you were sitting beside me at that bingo table last night you would have seen Gazelle Nataways win that big pot again with your own two eyes.

ANNIE:

Emily Dictionary and I went to Little Current to listen to Fritz the Katz.

PELAJIA:

What in God's name kind of a band might that be?

ANNIE:

Country rock. My favorite. Fritz the Katz is from Toronto.

PELAJIA:

Fritzy ... ritzy ... Philomena! Say something.

PHILOMENA:

My record player is in Espanola getting fixed.

ANNIE:

That's nice.

PHILOMENA:

Good.

ANNIE:

Is it true Gazelle Nataways plans to spend her bingo money to go to Toronto with ... with Big Joey?

PHILOMENA:

Who wants to know? Emily Dictionary?

ANNIE:

I guess so.

PELAJIA:

That Gazelle Nataways gonna leave all her babies behind and let them starve to death?

ANNIE:

I guess so. I don't know. I'm asking you.

11

PELAJIA and PHILOMENA:

We don't know.

ANNIE:

I'm on my way to Marie-Adele's to pick her up.

PELAJIA:

Why? Where you gonna put her down?

Pelajia and Philomena laugh.

ANNIE:

I mean, we're going to the store together. To the post office. We're going to pick up a parcel. They say there's a parcel for me. They say it's shaped like a record. And they say it's from Sudbury. So it must be from my daughter, Ellen . . .

PELAJIA and PHILOMENA:

. . . "who lives with this white guy in Sudbury" . . .

ANNIE:

How did you know?

PHILOMENA:

Everybody knows.

ANNIE:

His name is Ray<u>mond</u>. Not <u>Ray</u>mond. But Ray<u>mond</u>. Like in Bon Bon.

Philomena tries out "bon bon" to herself.

He's French.

PELAJIA:

Oh?

ANNIE:

Garage mechanic. He fixes cars. And you know, talking about Frenchmen, that old priest is holding another bingo next week and when I win . . .

To Philomena.

Are you going?

PELAJIA:

Does a bear shit in the woods?

ANNIE:

. . . when I win, I'm going to Espanola and play the bingo there. Emily Dictionary says that Fire Minklater can give us a ride in her new car. She got it through Raymond's garage. The bingo in Espanola is bigger. And it's better. And I'll win. And then I'll go to Sudbury, where the bingos are even bigger and better. And then I can visit my daughter, Ellen . . .

PELAJIA:

. . . "who lives with this white guy in Sudbury" . . .

ANNIE:

. . . and go shopping in the record stores and go to the hotel and drink beer quietly - not noisy and crazy like here - and listen to the live bands. It will be so much fun. I hope Emily Dictionary can come with me.

PHILOMENA:

It's true. I've been thinking ...

PELAJIA:

You don't say.

PHILOMENA:

It's true. The bingos here are getting kind of boring ...

ANNIE:

That old priest is too slow and sometimes he gets the numbers all mixed up and the pot's not big enough.

PHILOMENA:

And I don't like the way he calls the numbers. *Nasally.* B 12, O 64.

ANNIE:

When Little Girl Manitowabi won last month ...

PHILOMENA:

She won just enough to take a taxi back to Buzwah.

ANNIE:

That's all.

> *Both Annie and Philomena pause to give a quick sigh of yearning.*

PHILOMENA:

Annie Cook, I want that big pot.

ANNIE:

We all want big pots.

PELAJIA:

Start a revolution!

PHILOMENA and ANNIE:

Yes!

ANNIE:

All us Wasy women. We'll march up the hill, burn the church hall down, scare the priest to death, and then we'll march all the way to Espanola, where the bingos are bigger and better . . .

PHILOMENA:

We'll hold big placards!

ANNIE:

They'll say: "Wasy women want bigger bingos!"

PELAJIA:

And one will say: "Annie Cook Wants Big Pot!"

PHILOMENA:

. . . and the numbers at those bingos in Espanola go faster and the pots get bigger by the week. Oh, Pelajia Patchnose, I'm getting excited just thinking about it!

ANNIE:

I'm going.

PELAJIA:

You are, are you?

ANNIE:

Yes. I'm going. I'm running out of time. I'm going to Marie-Adele's house and then we'll walk to the store together to pick up the parcel - I'm sure there'll be a letter in it, and Marie-Adele is expecting mail, too - and we'll see if Emily Dictionary is working today and we'll ask her if Fire Minklater has her new car yet so we can go to Espanola for that big pot.

She begins to descend the ladder.

PELAJIA:

Well, you don't have much to do today, do you?

ANNIE:

Well. Toodle-oo!

And she pops down the ladder and is gone.

PELAJIA:

Not bad for someone who was in such a hurry to get her parcel. She talks faster than she walks.

Noticing how dejected and abandoned Philomena looks, she holds up her hammer.

Bingo money. Top quality. $24.95.

PHILOMENA:

It's true. Bingos here in Wasy are getting smaller and smaller all the time. Especially now when the value of the dollar is getting lesser and lesser. In the old days, when Bingo Betty was still alive and walking these dirt roads, she'd come to every single bingo and she'd sit there like the Queen of Tonga, big and huge like a roast

16

beef, smack-dab in the middle of the bingo hall. One night, I remember, she brought two young cousins from the city - two young women, dressed real fancy, like they were going to Sunday church - and Bingo Betty made them sit one on her left, with her three little bingo cards, and one on her right, with her three little ones. And Bingo Betty herself sat in the middle with 27 cards. Twenty seven cards! Amazing.

Pelajia starts to descend the ladder, and Philomena, getting excited, steps closer and closer to the edge of the roof.

And those were the days when they still used bingo chips, not these dabbers like nowadays, and everyone came with a little margarine container full of these bingo chips. When the game began and they started calling out the numbers, Bingo Betty was all set, like a horse at the race-track in Sudbury, you could practically see the foam sizzling and bubbling between her teeth. Bingo Betty! Bingo Betty with her beady little darting eyes, sharp as needles, and her roly-poly jiggledy-piggledy arms with their stubby little claws would go: chiga-chiga-chiga-chiga-chiga-chiga arms flying across the table smooth as angel's wings chiga-chiga-chiga-chiga-chiga-chiga-woosh! Cousin on the left chiga-chiga, cousin on the right chiga, chiga-eeee!

She narrowly misses falling off the roof and cries out in terror.

PELAJIA:
Philomena!

PHILOMENA:

> *Scrambling on hands and knees to Pelajia, and coming to rest in this languorous pose, takes a moment to regain her composure and catch her breath.*

And you know, to this very day, they say that on certain nights at the bingo here in Wasy, they say you can see Bingo Betty's ghost, like a mist, hovering in the air above the bingo tables, playing bingo like it's never been played before. Or since.

PELAJIA:

Amazing! She should have gone to Toronto.

> *Black-out.*

> *The same day, same time, in Wasaychigan Hill. Marie-Adele Starblanket is standing alone outside her house, in her yard, by her 14-post white picket fence. Her house is down the hill from Pelajia Patchnose's, close to the lake. A seagull watches her from a distance away. He is the dancer in white feathers. Through this whole section, Nanabush (i.e. Nanabush in the guise of the seagull), Marie-Adele, and Zhaboonigan play "games" with each other. Only she and Zhaboonigan Peterson can see the spirit inside the bird and can sort of (though not quite) recognize him for who he is. A doll belonging to a little girl lies on the porch floor. Marie-Adele throws little stones at the seagull.*

MARIE-ADELE:

Awus! Wee-chee-gis. Ka-tha pu-g'wun-ta oo-ta pee-wee-sta-ta-gu-mik-si. Awus! Neee. U-wi-nuk oo-ma kee-tha ee-tee-thi-mi-soo-yin holy spirit chee? Awus! Hey, maw ma-a oop-mee tay-si-thow u-wu seagull bird. I-goo-ta poo-goo ta-poo. Nu-gu-na-wa-pa-mik. Nu-gu-na-wa-pa-mik.

NANABUSH:

As-tum.

MARIE-ADELE:

Neee. Moo-tha ni-gus-kee-tan tu-pi-mi-tha-an. Moo-tha oo-ta-ta-gwu-na n'tay-yan. Chees-kwa. *Pause.* Ma-ti poo-ni-mee-see i-goo-ta wee-chi-gi-seagull bird come shit on my fence one more time and you and anybody else look like you cook like stew on my stove. Awus![2]

Veronique St. Pierre "passes by" with her adopted daughter Zhaboonigan Peterson.

VERONIQUE:

Talking to the birds again, Marie-Adele Starblanket?

---

2 **Marie-Adele:** Go away! You stinking thing. Don't coming messing around here for nothing. Go away! Neee. Who the hell do you think you are, the Holy Spirit? Go away! Hey, but he won't fly away, this seagull bird. He just sits there. And watches me. Watches me.
Nanabush: Come.
Marie-Adele: Neee. I can't fly away. I have no wings. Yet. *Pause.* Will you stop shitting all over the place you stinking seagull bird etc. (Cree).
(Note: "Neee" is a very common Cree expression with the approximate meaning of "Oh you.")

19

MARIE-ADELE:

Aha. Veronique St. Pierre. How are you today?

VERONIQUE:

Black Lady Halked's sister-in-law Fire Minklater, Fire Minklater's husband, just bought Fire Minklater a car in Sudbury.

MARIE-ADELE:

New?

VERONIQUE:

Used. They say he bought it from some Frenchman, some garage. Cray-<u>on</u>.

MARIE-ADELE:

Ray<u>mond</u>.

VERONIQUE:

These Frenchmen are forever selling us their used cars. And I'm sure that's why Black Lady Halked has been baring those big yellow teeth of hers, smiling all over the reserve recently. She looks like a hound about to pounce on a mouse, she smiles so hard when she smiles. I'd like to see her smile after plastic surgery. Anyway. At the bingo last night she was hinting that it wouldn't be too long before she would be able to go to the bingo in Espanola more frequently. Unfortunately, a new game started and you know how Black Lady Halked has to concentrate when she plays bingo - her forehead looks like corduroy, she concentrates so hard - so I didn't get a chance to ask her what she meant. So. Fire Minklater has a used car. Imagine! Maybe I can make friends with her again. NO! I wouldn't be caught dead inside her car.

Not even if she had a brand-new Cadillac. How are your
children? All 14 of them.

MARIE-ADELE:

Okay, I guess.

VERONIQUE:

Imagine. And all from one father. Anyway. Who will
take care of them after you . . . ahem . . . I mean . . .
when you go to the hospital?

MARIE-ADELE:

Eugene.

ZHABOONIGAN:

Is he gentle?

MARIE-ADELE:

Baby-cakes. How are you?

ZHABOONIGAN:

Fine.

Giggles.

VERONIQUE:

She's fine. She went berry-picking yesterday with the
children.

ZHABOONIGAN:

Where's Nicky?

MARIE-ADELE:

Nicky's down at the beach.

ZHABOONIGAN:
Why?

MARIE-ADELE:
Taking care of Rose-Marie.

ZHABOONIGAN:
Oh.

MARIE-ADELE:
Yup.

ZHABOONIGAN:
Me and Nicky, ever lots of blueberries!

MARIE-ADELE:
Me and Nicky picked lots of blueberries.

ZHABOONIGAN:
I didn't see you there.

MARIE-ADELE:
When?

ZHABOONIGAN:
Before today.

MARIE-ADELE:
How come Nicky didn't come home with any?

ZHABOONIGAN:
Why?

Marie-Adele shrugs. Zhaboonigan imitates this, and then pretends she is stuffing her mouth with berries.

MARIE-ADELE:
Aw, yous went and made pigs of yourselves.

ZHABOONIGAN:
Nicky's the pig.

MARIE-ADELE:
Neee.

ZHABOONIGAN:
Are you going away far?

MARIE-ADELE:
I'm not going far.

ZHABOONIGAN:
Oh. Are you pretty?

Marie-Adele, embarrassed for a moment, smiles and Zhaboonigan smiles, too.

MARIE-ADELE:
You're pretty, too.

Zhaboonigan tugs at Marie-Adele's shoelaces.

Oh, Zhaboonigan. Now you have to tie it up. I can't bend too far cuz I get tired.

Zhaboonigan tries to tie the shoelaces with great difficulty. When she finds she can't she throws her arms up and screams.

ZHABOONIGAN:
Dirty trick! Dirty trick!

She bites her hand and hurts herself.

MARIE-ADELE:
Now, don't get mad.

VERONIQUE:
Stop it. Stop it right now.

ZHABOONIGAN:
No! No!

MARIE-ADELE:
Zha. Zha. Listen. Listen.

ZHABOONIGAN:
Stop it! Stop it right now!

MARIE-ADELE:
Come on Zha. You and I can name the koo-koos-suk.[3] All 14 of them.

ZHABOONIGAN:
Okay. Here we go.

---

3 The little pigs. (Cree)

*Marie-Adele leads Zhaboonigan over to the pick-
et fence and Veronique follows them.*

ZHABOONIGAN:
> *To Veronique.*

No.

> *Veronique retreats, obviously hurt.*

MARIE-ADELE:
> *Taking Zhaboonigan's hand and counting on the
> 14 posts of her white picket fence.*

Simon, Andrew, Matthew, Janie, Nicky, Ricky, Ben, Mark,
Ron, Don, John, Tom, Pete, and Rose-Marie. There.

> *Underneath Marie-Adele's voice, Zhaboonigan has
> been counting.*

ZHABOONIGAN:
One, two, three, four, five, six, seven, eight, nine, ten,
eleven, twelve, thirteen, fourteen.

> *Giggles.*

MARIE-ADELE:
Ever good counter you, Zhaboonigan.

ZHABOONIGAN:
Yup.

VERONIQUE:

This reserve, sometimes I get so sick of it. They laugh at me behind my back, I just know it. They laugh at me and Pierre St. Pierre because we don't have any children of our own. "Imagine, they say, she's on her second husband already and she still can't have children!" They laugh at Zhaboonigan Peterson because she's crazy, that's what they call her. They can't even take care of their own people, they'd rather laugh at them. I'm the only person who would take Zhaboonigan after her parents died in that horrible car crash near Manitowaning on Saturday November 12 1964 may they rest in peace *She makes a quick sign of the cross without skipping a beat.* I'm the only one around here who is kind enough. And they laugh at me. Oh, I wish I had a new stove, Marie-Adele. My stove is so old and broken down, only two elements work anymore and my oven is starting to talk back at me.

MARIE-ADELE:

Get it fixed.

VERONIQUE:

You know that Pierre St. Pierre never has any money. He drinks it all up.

She sighs longingly.

Some day! Anyway. Zhaboonigan here wanted to go for a swim so I thought I'd walk her down - drop by and see how you and the children are doing - it will do my weak heart good, I was saying to myself.

MARIE-ADELE:

Awus!

26

*As she throws a pebble at the seagull on the stone,
Veronique, for a second, thinks it's her Marie-
Adele is shooing away. There is a brief silence
broken after awhile by Zhaboonigan's little giggle.*

VERONIQUE:

Anyway. I was walking down by that Big Joey's shame-
less little shack just this morning when guess who pokes
her nose out the window but Gazelle Nataways - the
nerve of that woman. I couldn't see inside but I'm sure
she was only half-dressed, her hairdo was all mixed up
and she said to me: "Did you know, Veronique St.
Pierre, that Little Girl Manitowabi told me her daughter, June
Bug McLeod, just got back from the hospital in Sudbury
where she had her tubes tied and told her that THE BIG-
GEST BINGO IN THE WORLD is coming to Toronto?"

MARIE-ADELE:

When?

VERONIQUE:

I just about had a heart attack.

MARIE-ADELE:

When?

VERONIQUE:

But I said to Gazelle anyway: Is there such a thing as
a BIGGEST BINGO IN THE WORLD? And she said:
Yes. And she should know about these things because
she spends all her waking and sleeping hours just banging about in bed with the biggest thing on Manitoulin
Island, I almost said.

27

MARIE-ADELE:
This bingo. When?

VERONIQUE:
She didn't know. And now that I think of it, I don't know whether to believe her. After all, who should believe a woman who wrestles around with dirt like Big Joey all night long leaving her poor babies to starve to death in her empty kitchen? But if it's true, Marie-Adele, if it's true that THE BIGGEST BINGO IN THE WORLD is coming to Toronto, I'm going and I want you to come with me.

MARIE-ADELE:
Well ...

VERONIQUE:
I want you to come shopping with me and help me choose my new stove after I win.

MARIE-ADELE:
Hang on ...

VERONIQUE:
They have good stoves in Toronto.

MARIE-ADELE:
Let's find out for sure. Then we start making plans.

VERONIQUE:
Maybe we should go back and ask that Gazelle Nataways about this. If she's sure.

MARIE-ADELE:

Maybe we should go and ask June Bug McLeod herself.

VERONIQUE:

We can't walk to Buzwah and I'm too old to hitch-hike.

MARIE-ADELE:

There's Eugene's van. He'll be home by six.

VERONIQUE:

I want to find out NOW. But what if people see us standing at Big Joey's door?

MARIE-ADELE:

What do you mean? We just knock on the door, march right in, ask the bitch, and march right out again.

VERONIQUE:

Zhaboonigan dear, wait for me over there.

She waits until Zhaboonigan is safely out of earshot and then leans over to Marie-Adele in a conspiratorial whisper.

Anyway. You must know, Marie-Adele, that there's all kinds of women who come streaming out of that house at all hours of the day and night. I might be considered one of them. You know your youngest sister, Emily Dictionary, was seen staggering out of that house in the dead of night two nights ago?

MARIE-ADELE:

Veronique St. Pierre, what Emily Dictionary does is Emily's business.

29

Annie Cook enters, walking fast and comes to a screeching halt.

ANNIE:

Hallooooo! Whatchyou doin'?

VERONIQUE:

Giving Annie the baleful eye.

How are you?

ANNIE:

High as a kite. Just kidding. Hi, Zha.

ZHABOONIGAN:

Hi.

Giggles. She runs toward Marie-Adele, bumping into Annie en route.

ANNIE:

Hey, Marie-Adele.

ZHABOONIGAN:

Marie-Adele. How's your cancer?

Giggles and scurries off laughing.

VERONIQUE:

Shkanah, Zhaboonigan, sna-ma-bah . . .[4]

---

4 Shush, Zhaboonigan, don't say that. (Ojibway)

MARIE-ADELE:

Come on, before the post office closes for lunch.

VERONIQUE:

You didn't tell me you were going to the store.

ANNIE:

Well, we are.

To Marie-Adele.

Hey, is Simon in? I'm sure he's got my Ricky Skaggs album. You know the one that goes *Sings.* "Honeee!"

Calling into the house.

Yoo-hoo, Simon!

MARIE-ADELE:

He's in Espanola with Eugene.

VERONIQUE:

Expecting mail, Annie Cook?

ANNIE:

A parcel from my daughter, Ellen, who lives with this white guy in Sudbury . . .

VERONIQUE:

So I've heard.

ANNIE:

And my sister here is expecting a letter, too.

VERONIQUE:

From whom?

ANNIE:

From the doctor, about her next check-up.

VERONIQUE:

When?

MARIE-ADELE:

We don't know when. Or where. Annie, let's go.

ANNIE:

They say it's shaped like a record.

VERONIQUE:

Maybe there'll be news in that parcel about THE BIG-GEST BINGO IN THE WORLD!

Shouts toward the lake, in a state of great excitement.

Zhaboonigan! Zhaboonigan! We're going to the store!

ANNIE:

THE BIGGEST BINGO IN THE WORLD?

VERONIQUE:

In Toronto. Soon. Imagine! Gazelle Nataways told me. She heard about it from Little Girl Manitowabi over in Buzwah who heard about it from her daughter June Bug McLeod who just got back from the hospital in Sudbury where she had her tubes tied I just about had a heart attack!

ANNIE:

Toronto?

MARIE-ADELE:

We gotta find out for sure.

ANNIE:

Right.

MARIE-ADELE:

We could go to Big Joey's and ask Gazelle Nataways except Veronique St. Pierre's too scared of Gazelle.

VERONIQUE:

I am not.

ANNIE:

You are too.

MARIE-ADELE:

We could wait and borrow Eugene's van ...

VERONIQUE:

I am not.

ANNIE:

... drive over to Buzwah ...

MARIE-ADELE:

... and ask June Bug McLeod ...

ANNIE:

... but wait a minute!...

MARIE-ADELE and ANNIE:

Maybe there IS news in that parcel about this BIGGEST
BINGO IN THE WORLD!

MARIE-ADELE:

Come on.

VERONIQUE:

Shouting toward the lake.

Zhaboonigan! Zhaboonigan!

ANNIE:

And here I was so excited about the next little bingo
that old priest is holding next week. Toronto! Oh, I hope
it's true!

VERONIQUE:

Zhaboonigan! Zhaboonigan! Zhaboonigan! Dammit!
We're going to the store!

And the "march" to the store begins, during which Nanabush, still in the guise of the seagull, follows them and continues to play tricks, mimicking their hand movements, the movement of their mouths, etc. The three women appear each in her own spot of light at widely divergent points on the stage area.

ANNIE:

When I go to the BIGGEST BINGO IN THE WORLD, in Toronto, I will win. For sure, I will win. If they shout the B 14 at the end, for sure I will win. The B 14 is my lucky number after all. Then I will take all my money and I will go to every record store in Toronto. I will buy every single one of Patsy Cline's records, especially the one that goes *Sings.* "I go a-walking, after midnight," oh I go crazy every time I hear that one. Then I will buy a huge record player, the biggest one in the whole world. And then I will go to all the taverns and all the night clubs in Toronto and listen to the live bands while I drink beer quietly - not noisy and crazy like here - I will bring my daughter Ellen and her white guy from Sudbury and we will sit together. Maybe I will call Fritz the Katz and he will take me out. Maybe he will hire me as one of his singers and I can *Sings.* "Oooh," in the background while my feet go *Shuffles her feet from side to side.* while Fritz the Katz is singing and the lights are flashing and the people are drinking beer and smoking cigarettes and dancing. Ohhh, I could dance all night with that Fritz the Katz. When I win, when I win THE BIGGEST BINGO IN THE WORLD!

MARIE-ADELE:

When I win THE BIGGEST BINGO IN THE WORLD,
I'm gonna buy me an island. In the North Channel, right
smack-dab in the middle - eem-shak min-stik[5] - the most
beautiful island in the world. And my island will have
lots of trees - great big bushy ones - and lots and lots
and lots of sweetgrass. MMMMM! And there's gonna be
pine trees and oak trees and maple trees and big stones
and little stonelets - neee - and, oh yeah, this real neat
picket fence, real high, long and very, very, very white.
No bird shit. Eugene will live there and me and all my
Starblanket kids. Yup, no more smelly, stinky old pulp
and paper mill in Espanola for my Eugene - pooh! - my
12 Starblanket boys and my two Starblanket girls and
me and my Eugene all living real nice and comfy right
there on Starblanket Island, the most beautiful incredible
goddamn island in the whole goddamn world. Eem-shak
min-stik! When I win THE BIGGEST BINGO IN THE
WORLD!

VERONIQUE:

Well, when I win the BIGGEST BINGO IN THE
WORLD. No! After I win THE BIGGEST BINGO IN
THE WORLD, I will go shopping for a brand-new stove.
In Toronto. At the Eaton Centre. A great big stove. The
kind Madame Benoit has. The kind that has the three
different compartments in the oven alone. I'll have the
biggest stove on the reserve. I'll cook for all the children
on the reserve. I'll adopt all of Marie-Adele Starblanket's
14 children and I will cook for them. I'll even cook for
Gazelle Nataways' poor starving babies while she's loll-
ing around like a pig in Big Joey's smelly, sweaty bed.
And Pierre St. Pierre can drink himself to death for all

---

5 A great big island. (Cree)

I care. Because I'll be the best cook on all of Manitoulin Island! I'll enter competitions. I'll go to Paris and meet what's-his-name Cordon Bleu! I'll write a cookbook called "The Joy of Veronique St. Pierre's Cooking" and it will sell in the millions! And I will become rich and famous! Zhaboonigan Peterson will wear a mink while she eats steak tartare-de-frou-frou! Madame Benoit will be so jealous she'll suicide herself. Oh, when I win THE BIGGEST BINGO IN THE WORLD!

Zhaboonigan comes running in from swimming, "chasing" after the other three women, counting to herself and giggling.

ZHABOONIGAN:

One, two, three, four, five, six, seven, eight, nine, ten, eleven, twelve, thirteen, fourteen.

At the store. Annie Cook, Marie-Adele Starblanket, Veronique St. Pierre, and Zhaboonigan Peterson have arrived. Emily Dictionary makes a sudden appearance, carrying a huge bag of flour on her shoulder. She is one tough lady, wearing cowboy boots, tight blue jeans, a black leather jacket - all three items worn to the seams - and she sports one black eye.

EMILY:

In a loud, booming voice that paralyzes all movement in the room while she speaks.

Zhaboonigan Peterson! What in Red Lucifer's name ever possessed you to be hangin' out with a buncha' dizzy old dames like this?

Bag of flour hits the floor with a "doof."

37

MARIE-ADELE:

Emily. Your eye.

EMILY:

Oh, bit of a tussle.

VERONIQUE:

With who?

EMILY:

None of your goddamn business.

MARIE-ADELE:

Emily, please.

ANNIE:

Following Emily about the store while Veronique tries, in vain, to hear what she can.

I wasn't able to find out from Pelajia Patchnose or Philomena Moosemeat if Gazelle Nataways is going to Toronto this weekend with ... Big Joey ... they didn't know ... Gazelle did win the bingo last night though.

EMILY:

Aw shit. Veronique St. Pierre, you old bag. Is it true Gazelle Nataways is takin' off for Toronto with that hunk Big Joey?

VERONIQUE:

It WAS you coming out of that house two nights ago. I walked by as quickly as I could ...

EMILY:

... shoulda come out and nailed your big floppy ears to the door ...

VERONIQUE:

... and I would have called the police but I was too scared Big Joey might come after me and Zhaboonigan later ...

EMILY:

... yeah, right.

ZHABOONIGAN:

Yeah, right.

VERONIQUE:

... and I have a weak heart, you know? Who hit you? Big Joey? Or Gazelle Nataways?

EMILY:

The nerve of this woman.

VERONIQUE:

Well?

EMILY:

Calls Zhaboonigan, who is behind the counter, on the floor, playing with the merchandise.

Zhaboonigan Peterson! Where in Red Lucifer's name is that dozy pagan?

VERONIQUE:

You keep hanging around that house and you're gonna end up in deep trouble. You don't know how wicked and vicious those Nataways women can get. They say there's witchcraft in their blood. And with manners like yours, Emily Dictionary, you'd deserve every hex you got.

EMILY:

Do I know this woman? Do I know this woman?

VERONIQUE:

During this speech, Marie-Adele and Annie sing "Honeee" tauntingly.

I'm sorry I have to say this in front of everyone like this but this woman has just accused my daughter of being a pagan. I didn't call her Zhaboonigan. The people on this reserve, who have nothing better to do with their time than call each other names, they called her that. Her name is Marie-Adele. Marie-Adele Peterson. You should talk. I should ask you where in Red ... Red ... whatever, you got a circus of a name like Emily Dictionary.

Emily grabs Veronique and throws her across the room. Veronique goes flying right into Pelajia, who has entered the store during the latter part of this speech.

PELAJIA:

Veronique St. Pierre! Control yourself or I'll hit you over the head with my hammer.

VERONIQUE:

Blows a "raspberry" in Pelajia's face.

Bleah!

ANNIE:

No, Pelajia, no.

EMILY:

Go ahead, Pelajia. Make my day.

ANNIE:

Down, put it down.

PHILOMENA:

As she comes scurrying into the store.

I have to use the toilet.

Running to Emily.

I have to use your toilet.

And goes scurrying into the toilet.

ANNIE:

To Pelajia.

Remember, that's Veronique St. Pierre and if you get on the wrong side of Veronique St. Pierre she's liable to spread rumors about you all over kingdom come and you'll lose every bit of respect you got on this reserve. Don't let those pants you're wearing go to your head.

PELAJIA:

Catching Annie by the arm as she tries to run away.

Annie Cook! You got a mouth on you like a helicopter.

ANNIE:

Veronique's mad at you, Emily, because you won't tell her what happened the other night at Big Joey's house. And she's jealous of Gazelle Nataways because Gazelle won the bingo again last night and she hopes you're the one person on this reserve who has the guts to stand up to Gazelle.

VERONIQUE:

Making a lunge at Annie, who hides behind Emily.

What's that! What's that! Ohhh! Ohhh!

ANNIE:

Leave me alone, you old snoop. All I wanna know is this big bingo really happening in Toronto.

VERONIQUE:

Annie Cook. You are a little suck.

EMILY:

To Veronique.

Someday, someone oughta stick a great big piece of shit into that mouth of yours.

PELAJIA:

To Emily.

And someday, someone ought to wash yours out with soap.

PHILOMENA:

Throwing the toilet door open, she sits there in her glory, panties down to her ankles.

Emily Dictionary. You come back to the reserve after all these years and you strut around like you own the place. I know Veronique St. Pierre is a pain in the ass but I don't care. She's your elder and you respect her. Now shut up, all of you, and let me shit in peace.

And slams the washroom door. Veronique, scandalized by this, haughtily walks through toward the door, bumping into Pelajia en route.

PELAJIA:

Philomena. Get your bum out here. Veronique St. Pierre is about to lose her life.

She raises her hammer at Veronique.

VERONIQUE:

To Pelajia.

Put that hammer away. And go put a skirt on, for heaven's sake, you look obscene in those tight pants.

ANNIE:

Hit her. Go on. Hit the bitch. One good bang is all she needs.

EMILY:

Yeah, right. A gang-bang is more like it.

43

And a full-scale riot breaks out, during which the women throw every conceivable insult at each other. Emily throws open the toilet door and Philomena comes stomping out, pulling her panties on and joining the riot. All talk at the same time, quietly at first, but then getting louder and louder until they are all screaming.

PHILOMENA:

To Annie. What a slime. Make promises and then you go do something else. And I always have to smile at you. What a slime. *To Emily.* All that tough talk. I know what's behind it all. You'll never be big enough to push me around. *To Marie-Adele.* Fourteen kids! You look like a wrinkled old prune already. *To Pelajia.* At least I'm a woman. *To Veronique.* Have you any idea how, just how offensive, how obnoxious you are to people? And that halitosis. Pooh! You wouldn't have it if you didn't talk so much.

EMILY:

To Philomena. So damned bossy and pushy and sucky. You make me sick. Always wanting your own way. *To Veronique.* Goddamned trouble-making old crow. *To Pelajia.* Fuckin' self-righteous old bitch. *To Marie-Adele.* Mental problems, that's what you got, princess. I ain't no baby. I'm the size of a fuckin' church. *To Annie.* You slippery little slut. Brain the size of a fuckin' pea. Fuck, man, take a Valium.

VERONIQUE:

To Emily. You have no morals at all. You sick pervert. You should have stayed where you came from, where all the other perverts are. *To Pelajia.* Slow turtle. Talk big and move like Jell-o. *To Annie.* Cockroach! *To Philomena.* You big phony. Flush yourself down that damned toilet of yours and shut up. *To Marie-Adele.* Hasn't this slimy little reptile *Referring to Annie.* ever told you that sweet little Ellen of hers is really Eugene's daughter? Go talk to the birds in Sudbury and find out for yourself.

PELAJIA:

To Veronique. This reserve would be a better place without you. I'm tired of dealing with people like you. Tired. *To Marie-Adele.* You can't act that way. This here's no time to be selfish. You spoiled brat. *To Philomena.* You old fool. I thought you were coming back to help me and here you are all trussed up like a Thanksgiving turkey, putting on these white lady airs. *To Annie.* Annie Cook. Move to Kapuskasing! *To Emily.* "Fuck, fuck, fuck!" Us Indian women got no business talking like that.

MARIE-ADELE:

To Pelajia. You don't have all the answers. You can't fix everything. *To Annie.* White guys. Slow down a minute and see how stupid you look. *To Emily.* Voice like a fog-horn. You ram through everything like a truck. You look like a truck. *To Veronique.* Some kind of insect, sticking insect claws into everybody's business. *To Philomena.* Those clothes. You look like a giant Kewpie doll. You make me laugh.

ANNIE:

> *To Marie-Adele.* You always make me feel so . . . small . . . like a little pig or something. You're no better than me. *To Philomena.* Why can't you go to bingo by yourself, you big baby? At least I got staying power. Piss off. *To Veronique.* Sucking off everybody else's life like a leech because you got nothing of your own. Pathetic old coot. Just buzz off. *To Emily.* You call me names. I don't call you names. You think you're too smart. Shut up. *To Pelajia.* "Queen of the Indians," you think that's what you are. Well, that stupid hammer of yours doesn't scare me. Go away. Piss me off.

> *Then Pelajia lifts her hammer with a big loud "Woah"! And they come to a sudden dead stop. Pause. Then one quick final volley, all at once, loudest of all.*

PHILOMENA:

> *To Annie.*

You slimy buck-toothed drunken worm!

EMILY:

> *To Veronique.*

Fuckin' instigator!

VERONIQUE:

> *To Marie-Adele.*

Clutching, clinging vine!

PELAJIA:

To Veronique.

Evil no-good insect!

MARIE-ADELE:

To Veronique.

Maggot-mouthed vulture!

ANNIE:

To Philomena.

Fat-assed floozy, get off the pot!

Marie-Adele, stung to the quick, makes a vicious grab for Veronique by the throat. In a split-second, all freeze. Lights out in store interior. Lights on on Zhaboonigan, who has run out in fright during the riot, outside the store. Nanabush, still in his guise as the seagull, makes a grab at Zhaboonigan. Zhaboonigan begins talking to the bird.

ZHABOONIGAN:

Are you gentle? I was not little. Maybe. Same size as now. Long ago it must be? You think I'm funny? Shhh. I know who you are. There, there. Boys. White boys. Two. Ever nice white wings, you. I was walking down the road to the store. They ask me if I want ride in car. Oh, I was happy I said, "Yup." Took me far away. Ever nice ride. Dizzy. They took all my clothes off me. Put something up inside me here. *Pointing to her crotch, underneath her dress.* Many, many times. Remember. Don't fly away. Don't go. I saw you before. There, there. It was a. Screwdriver. They put the screwdriver

47

inside me. Here. Remember. Ever lots of blood. The two white boys. Left me in the bush. Alone. It was cold. And then. Remember. Zhaboonigan. Everybody calls me Zhaboonigan. Why? It means needle. Zhaboonigan. Going-through-thing. Needle Peterson. Going-through-thing Peterson. That's me. It was the screwdriver. Nice. Nice. Nicky Ricky Ben Mark. *As she counts, with each name, feathers on the bird's wing.* Ever nice. Nice white birdie you.

> *During this last speech, Nanabush goes through agonizing contortions. Then lights change instantly back to the interior of the store. The six women spring back into action. Philomena stomps back into the toilet.*

MARIE-ADELE:

> *To Veronique.*

Fine. And the whole reserve knows the only reason you ever adopted Zhaboonigan is for her disability cheque.

ANNIE:

You fake saint.

> *Annie, Marie-Adele, and Emily start pushing Veronique, round-robin, between the three of them, laughing tauntingly until Veronique is almost reduced to tears.*

VERONIQUE:

> *Almost weeping.*

Bastards. The three of you.

Marie-Adele grabs Veronique by the throat and lifts her fist to punch her in the face. But the exertion causes her body to weaken, almost to the point of collapse, from her illness. At this point, Philomena emerges from the toilet.

PHILOMENA:
Crinkling her nose.

Emily. Your toilet.

WOMEN:
Shhhh.

MARIE-ADELE:
Holding her waist, reeling, barely audible.

Oh, shit.

PHILOMENA:
I can't get it to flush.

WOMEN:
Shhhh.

PELAJIA:
Rushing to Marie-Adele.

Marie-Adele. You're not well.

MARIE-ADELE:
Screams.

Don't touch me.

49

Complete silence from all while Marie-Adele weaves and struggles to keep herself from collapsing. Annie scurries offstage, to the back part of the store, where the post office would be.

EMILY:

To Veronique.

You f'in' bitch!

PHILOMENA:

What did I just tell you? Who did that to your eye?

VERONIQUE:

Big Joey.

EMILY:

To Veronique.

Look here, you old buzzard. I'll tell you a few things. You see this fist? You see these knuckles? You wanna know where they come from? Ten years. Every second night for 10 long ass-fuckin' years that goddamn Yellowknife asshole Henry Dadzinanare come home to me so drunk his eyes was spittin' blood like Red Lucifer himself and he'd beat me purple.

VERONIQUE:

I wish I'd been there to see it all.

EMILY:

Yeah, scumbag. I wish you'd been there to watch me learn to fight back like you've never seen a woman fight for her life before. Take a look at this eye. I earned it, Veronique St. Pierre, I earned it.

PHILOMENA:

Henry Dadzinanare, Big Joey. They're all the same. Emily, use your brains.

EMILY:

Use my brains. Yeah, right. I used them alright the night he came at me with an axe and just about sank it into my spine, I grabbed one bag, took one last look at the kids and walked out of his life forever.

ANNIE:

From offstage.

And she took the bus to San Francisco.

PHILOMENA:

And gets herself mixed up with a motorcycle gang, for God's sake.

EMILY:

Now addressing all in the room.

Rosabella Baez, Hortensia Colorado, Liz Jones, Pussy Commanda. And me. The best. "Rose and the Rez Sisters," that's us. And man, us sisters could weave knuckle magic.

VERONIQUE:

So why did you bother coming back?

51

PHILOMENA:

You stay out of this.

EMILY:

Come back to the Rez for a visit, get all wedged up with that hunk Big Joey one night ...

Grunts.

PHILOMENA:

I give up.

EMILY:

... and I was hooked. Couldn't leave. Settlin' back on a coupla beers with Big Joey the other night when Gazelle Nataways come sashayin' in like she's got half the Rez squished down the crack of her ass. She was high. I was high. Hell, we were all high. Get into a bit of a discussion, when she gets me miffed and I let fly, she let fly, Big Joey let fly, misses that nympho and lands me one in the eye instead.

VERONIQUE:

So it was Big Joey.

EMILY:

Damn rights. And that's as close as he got cuz I put him out for the night right then and there. Just one of these. *Brandishing her fist.* One. That's all it took.

Veronique runs off to look for Zhaboonigan.

ANNIE and PHILOMENA:

Emily Dictionary.

Philomena with exasperation, Annie with adulation, from offstage.

ANNIE:

You're amazing!

EMILY:

Not Dictionary. Dadzinanare. Henry Dadzinanare. The man who made me learn to fight back. Never let a man raise one dick hair against me since.

VERONIQUE:

Calling out to Zhaboonigan.

Zhaboonigan. Don't you be talking to the birds like that again. You're crazy enough as it is.

ANNIE:

As she comes running back in from the post office with her parcel, already unwrapped, and two letters, one for herself, already unfolded, and one still in its envelope.

See? I told you. It's a record. Patsy Cline.

PHILOMENA:

Never mind Patsy Cline.

ANNIE:

> *As she hands Marie-Adele the letter in the envelope.*

Hey, Marie-Adele.

EMILY:

Read your friggin' letter, Annie Cook.

ANNIE:

Listen to this.

> *Zhaboonigan walks back in as Annie reads her own letter very haltingly.*

Dear Mom: Here is the record you wanted. I thought you'd like the picture of Patsy Cline on the cover. *Annie shows off her record.* See? It's Patsy Cline. *Returns to her letter.* I also thought you might like to know that there is a bingo called THE BIGGEST BINGO IN THE WORLD. Can you fu ... ture that?

EMILY:

> *Who has been looking over Annie's shoulder.*

Feature. Feature.

ANNIE:

Can you ... feature ... that? ... that's coming to Toronto. The jackpot is $500,000. It's on Saturday, September 8. Raymond's Mom was in Toronto. Aunt Philomena will hit the roof when she hears this. Much love, your daughter Ellen.

> *Annie announces once more.*

There is a brief electric silence followed by an equally electric scream from all the women. Even Zhaboonigan screams. Excitement takes over completely.

VERONIQUE:

So it's true! It's true!

PHILOMENA:

The Espanola bingo. Piffle. Mere piffle.

VERONIQUE:

My new stove!

PHILOMENA:

My new toilet! White! Spirit white!

EMILY:

Grabbing Zhaboonigan and dancing around the room with her.

I'd take the money, come back to the Rez, beat the shit out of Gazelle Nataways and take you down to Frisco with me. Whaddaya think?

ZHABOONIGAN:

Yup.

MARIE-ADELE:

In the background, where she has been reading her letter quietly to herself.

September 10.

ANNIE:

Taking the letter from Marie-Adele.

Look, Pelajia. Marie-Adele's tests are in Toronto just two days after THE BIGGEST.

There is a brief embarrassed silence.

MARIE-ADELE:

Kill two birds with one stone.

To Nanabush.

I wanna go.

To Pelajia and Philomena.

I wanna go.

VERONIQUE:

Goood!

EMILY:

Mimicking Veronique.

Goood! Now how the hell are you guys gonna get down to Toronto? You're all goddamn welfare cases.

ANNIE:

Fire Minklater.

VERONIQUE:

Mary, mother of Jesus! I refuse, I absolutely refuse to be seen anywhere near that sorceress! We'll chip in and rent a car.

EMILY:

Zhaboonigan Peterson here gonna chauffeur you down?

ZHABOONIGAN:

Yup.

VERONIQUE:

Don't you make fun of my daughter.

EMILY:

What kind of stove you gonna buy, Veronique St. Pierre? Westinghouse? Electrolux? Yamaha? Kawasaki?

VERONIQUE:

Oh my god, Marie-Adele, I never thought about it. They will have so many stoves in Toronto, I'll get confused.

ANNIE:

If you go to Toronto and leave Wasy for even one day, Emily, you'll lose Big Joey forever ...

VERONIQUE:

To that witch!

ANNIE:

... and then whose thighs will you have to wrestle around with in the dead of night? You'll dry up, get all puckered up and pass into ancient history.

EMILY:

. Annie Cook. I don't know what the fuck you're yatterin' on about now but I'd like to hear you say two words of French to that white guy in Sudbury you're so damn proud of.

ANNIE:

Oh my god, Marie-Adele, she's right. I won't know what to say to this Ray<u>mond</u>. I've never met him. I can't speak French. All I can say in French is Ray<u>mond</u> and Bon Bon and I don't even know what that means. I can't go and live with them, not even after I win THE BIG-GEST BINGO IN THE WORLD. What am I gonna do?

She collapses on the floor and rolls around for a bit.

EMILY:

And Philomena Moosemeat's so fulla shit she'd need five toilets to get it all out.

PHILOMENA:

Going at Emily.

And just who do you think you're talking to, Miss Dictionary, just who the hell do you think you're talking to?

With a resounding belly butt from Emily, they begin to wrestle.

PELAJIA:

Banging her hammer on the counter.

Alright, alright. It's obvious we've got a problem here.

EMILY:

Throwing Philomena off to the side.

I'll say.

MARIE-ADELE:

It's true. None of us has any money.

But Veronique, standing behind Pelajia, winks at the others and makes a hand motion indicating that Pelajia, for one, does have money. All the other women slowly surround Pelajia. But Pelajia catches the drift and quickly collects herself to meet the onslaught. During Pelajia's speech, the women respond at periodic intervals with a "yoah" and "hmmm," etc., as when a chief speaks at a council meeting.

PELAJIA:

I say we all march down to the Band Office and ask the Band Council for a loan that will pay for the trip to this bingo. I know how to handle that tired old chief. He and I have been arguing about paved roads for years now. I'll tell him we'll build paved roads all over the reserve with our prize money. I'll tell him the people will stop drinking themselves to death because they'll have paved roads to walk on. I'll tell him there'll be more jobs because the people will have paved roads to drive to work on. I'll tell him the people will stop fighting and screwing around and Nanabush will come back to us because he'll have paved roads to dance on. There's enough money in there for everyone, I'll say. And if he doesn't lend us the money, I'll tell him I'm packing my bags and moving to Toronto tomorrow.

EMILY:

That oughta twist his arm but good.

PELAJIA:

And if he still says no, I'll bop him over the head with my hammer and we'll attack the accountant and take the money ourselves. Philomena, we're going to Toronto!

The seven women have this grand and ridiculous march to the band office, around the set and all over the stage area, with Pelajia leading them forward heroically, her hammer just a-swinging in the air. Nanabush trails merrily along in the rear of the line. They reach the "band office" - standing in one straight line square in front of the audience. The "invisible" chief "speaks": cacophonous percussion for about seven beats, the women listening more and more incredulously. Finally, the percussion comes to a dead stop.

PELAJIA:

No?

Pelajia raises her hammer to hit the "invisible" chief, Nanabush shrugs a "don't ask me, I don't know," Emily fingers a "fuck you, man." Blackout. End of Act One.

Act Two

All seven women are holding a meeting in the basement of Pelajia Patchnose's house. This is a collection of chairs and stools off to the side of the stage area. The only light comes from an old, beat-up trilight pole lamp. Some have tea, Emily and Annie a beer.

VERONIQUE:

We should have met at the priest's house.

PELAJIA:

No! We're gonna work this out on our own. Right here. Emily Dictionary, you chair.

And she lends Emily her hammer.

VERONIQUE:

She's good at ordering people around.

PHILOMENA:

Shut up.

EMILY:

First. When are we leaving?

She bangs the hammer regularly throughout the meeting.

VERONIQUE:

How much is the trip going to cost?

EMILY:

When are we leaving?

PHILOMENA:

How long to Toronto?

ANNIE:

Four hours.

EMILY:

When are we leaving?

PHILOMENA:

The only human being who can make it in four hours is Annie Cook.

VERONIQUE:

I'm not dying on the highway.

PHILOMENA:

Eight hours.

PELAJIA:

No way we're gonna stop at every toilet on the highway.

MARIE-ADELE:

Six hours. Eugene's driven there.

VERONIQUE:

Maybe we can borrow his van.

ANNIE:

Maybe we can borrow Big Joey's van.

A quick little aside to Pelajia.

Hey, can I have another beer?

PELAJIA:

No.

VERONIQUE:
What about Gazelle Nataways?

EMILY:
We're gonna borrow his van, not his buns, for Chris'sakes.

MARIE-ADELE:
The only thing we have to pay for is gas.

ANNIE:
Philomena's got gas.

EMILY:
Right! Six hours. Eugene's van.

MARIE-ADELE:
We still don't know when we're leaving.

PHILOMENA:
Bingo's on Saturday night.

ANNIE:
Leave Saturday morning.

VERONIQUE:
Oh! I'll be so tired for the bingo. I'll get confused. Wednesday. Rest on Thursday.

ANNIE:
And rest again on Friday? Too much resting. I can't go for that.

PELAJIA:

And we can't afford such a long stay.

PHILOMENA:

Where are we gonna stay?

EMILY:

Whoa!

Pause.

PELAJIA:

Friday night.

EMILY:

Right. Leave Friday night. Next.

PHILOMENA:

Coming home right after the bingo.

MARIE-ADELE:

And leave me behind? Remember my tests Monday morning.

EMILY:

Right. Monday noon, we come back. Next.

VERONIQUE:

Don't go so fast. My mind is getting confused.

EMILY:

Goood! Next.

MARIE-ADELE:
Where are we gonna stay?

ANNIE:
The Silver Dollar!

MARIE-ADELE:
You can't stay there.

ANNIE:
There's rooms upstairs.

PELAJIA:
You wanna sleep in a whorehouse?

VERONIQUE:
Zhaboonigan! Don't listen to this part.

PELAJIA:
There's room at my son's.

PHILOMENA:
Two washrooms! He's got a wonderful education.

EMILY:
Next.

VERONIQUE:
Who's going to drive?

ANNIE:
Emily. She can drive anything.

VERONIQUE:
I believe it.

ANNIE:
But I can drive, too.

VERONIQUE:
Oh my god.

ANNIE:
Long as I don't have to drive in the city. You drive the city.

VERONIQUE:
Me?

ANNIE and MARIE-ADELE:
No!

PELAJIA:
Long as you don't drive too fast, Annie Cook.

PHILOMENA:
And we'll pack a lunch for the trip and then eat in restaurants. Chinese.

PELAJIA:
Can't afford it. We chip in, buy groceries and cook at my son's.

VERONIQUE:
I'll give $10.

EMILY:

You old fossil. You want us to starve?

PHILOMENA:

$50 a day. Each.

EMILY:

Philomena Moosemeat! That's $50 times seven people times four days. That's over $1,000 worth of groceries.

VERONIQUE:

Imagine!

MARIE-ADELE:

Okay. Veronique St. Pierre. You cook. $20 apiece. Right?

EMILY:

Right. Next.

PHILOMENA:

Anybody writing this down?

ANNIE:

I'm gonna go to Sam the Recordman.

MARIE-ADELE:

I'll make the grocery list.

PELAJIA:

How much for gas?

VERONIQUE:

Still in dreamland over the groceries.

68

$1,000!

PHILOMENA:
> *Flabbergasted.*

Nooo! You goose.

ANNIE:
$40.

EMILY:
$150. Period. Next.

PELAJIA:
We got 10 days to find this money.

MARIE-ADELE:
What's it cost to get into the bingo?

VERONIQUE:
All the Indians in the world will be there!

PHILOMENA:
$50.

ANNIE:
And we're gonna be the only Indians there.

PELAJIA:
Silence.

There is a long, thoughtful silence, broken only
after awhile by a scream from Zhaboonigan.
Nanabush has knocked her off her stool. The
women laugh.

Can't think of anything else.

PHILOMENA:
Add it up.

She hands a pencil to Emily.

EMILY:
Calculates.

$1,400. You guys need $200 each.

VERONIQUE:
Where am I going to get $400?

EMILY:
Make it. End of meeting.

And the women start their fundraising activities
with a vengeance. The drive is underlined by a
wild rhythmic beat from the musician, one that
gets wilder and wilder with each successive beat,
though always underpinned by this persistent, al-
most dance-like pulse. The movement of the women
covers the entire stage area, and like the music,
gets wilder and wilder, until by the end it is as if
we are looking at an insane eight-ring circus,
eight-ring because through all this, Nanabush, as
the seagull, has a holiday, particularly with Marie-
Adele's lines of laundry, as Marie-Adele madly

70

strings one line of laundry after another all over the set, from Pelajia's roof to Emily's store, etc. For the garage sale, Annie sells off Pelajia's lamp, chairs, etc., so that Pelajia's "basement" simply dissolves into the madness of the fundraising drive.

Beat one.

Pelajia is hammering on the roof.
Emily is at the store cash register and rings up each sale as Annie, Philomena, Marie-Adele, Zhaboonigan, and Veronique stand shoulder to shoulder and pass the following from one side of the stage to the other:
seven large sacks marked "FLOUR"
two giant tubs marked "LARD"
one bushel of apples

Beat two.

Zhaboonigan brings small table on and puts it stage left.
Annie brings table on and puts it stage right.
Philomena brings a basket full of beer bottles to center and empties it. She has a baby attached to her.
Veronique comes on with cloth and Windex and starts "cleaning windows" rhythmically, listening to whatever gossip she can hear.
Marie-Adele strings two lines of clothing across the stage.
Pelajia hammers on her roof.
Emily brings on several empty beer cases and fills them with Philomena's bottles.

Beat three.

71

*Zhaboonigan brings in six quarts of blueberries
and then takes over window cleaning from Veronique.
Annie brings on basket of old clothes and a broken
kitchen chair.
Philomena brings on another basket full of beer
bottles, empties it. She now has two babies attached to her, like a fungus.
Emily fills beer cases rapidly, expertly.
Pelajia gets down off roof, hammering everything
until she is on hands and knees, hammering the
floor.
Marie-Adele strings third and fourth lines of
laundry across the stage.
Veronique comes in burdened with seven apple
pies and puts them on Annie's table.*

Beat four.

*Pelajia hammers as she crawls across the floor.
Zhaboonigan washes windows like a person possessed.
Emily runs and rings up a sale on the cash register
and then brings on more empty beer cases and
loads them up.
Philomena brings on a third load of bottles. Three
babies are now attached to her.
Annie brings on an old trilight pole lamp and an
old record player, which she opens and stacks
alongside the rest of her stuff.
Annie and Emily sing a line of their song with
very bad harmony.
Marie-Adele strings fifth and sixth lines of laundry
across stage.
Veronique comes on with seven loaves of bread
and puts them neatly by the pies.*

72

Beat five.

Pelajia hammers as she crawls across the floor, hammering everything in sight. The women protect their poor feet.
Zhaboonigan washes windows even faster; she's starting to cry.
Emily and Philomena work together filling the empty beer cases as fast as they can. Emily runs to the register, rings in seven sales and sings a bit of song with Annie, better this time. Philomena now has four kids attached to her body.
Annie comes on with a small black and white TV with rabbit ears and an old toaster.
Veronique comes on with six dozen buns and dumps them out of their tins all over the table.
Pelajia hammers faster and faster.
Zhaboonigan is now working like a maniac and is sobbing.
Marie-Adele strings seventh and eighth lines of laundry across stage.

Beat six.

Emily goes to cash register and tallies their earnings; she works the register with tremendous speed and efficiency all this beat.
Zhaboonigan continues washing windows.
Philomena sticks a sign in beer bottles: World's Biggest Bottle Drive. She now has five babies attached to her.
Veronique sticks a sign on her table: World's Biggest Bake Sale.
Annie sticks a sign up around her stuff: World's Biggest Garage Sale.
Marie-Adele sticks a sign up on Zha's table: Big Blueberries and Laundry While You Wait.

Pelajia begins hammering the air. She may have lost her marbles.

Beat Seven.

EMILY:

Whoa!

The "music" comes to a sudden stop. The women all collapse. The women look at each other. They then quickly clear the stage of everything they've brought on as Pelajia speaks, consulting her list. By the end of Pelajia's speech, the stage area is clear once more, except for a microphone stand that one of the women has brought on as part of the "clean-up" activities.

PELAJIA:

Bottle drive. Ten cents a bottle, 24 bottles a case, equals two dollars and 40 cents. 777 bottles collected divided by 24 is 32 cases and nine singles that's 32 times $2.40 equals $77.70. Blueberries equals $90. Good pickin' Zha and the Starblanket kids. Washing windows at $5.00 a house times 18 houses. Five eights are 40, carry the four and add the five is 90 bucks less two on account of that cheap Gazelle Nataways only gave three dollars. That's $88. Household repairs is four roofs including the Chief's and one tiled floor is $225. Garage sale brung in $246.95, the bake sale equals $83 after expenses, we make 110 bucks on doing laundry, 65 bucks babysitting, 145 from Emily doing a double shift at the store and I have generously donated $103 from my savings. That brings us to a grand total of $1233.65. So!

Emily and Annie move forward as the music starts up. They are lit only by tacky floor flood-lighting, and are, in effect, at the Anchor Inn, Little Current. Emily speaks into the microphone.

EMILY:

Thank-you. Thank-you, ladies and gentlemen. I thank you very much. And now for the last song of the night, ladies and gents, before we hit the road. A song that's real special to me in my heart. A song I wrote in memory of one Rosabella Baez, a Rez Sister from way back. And Rose baby, if you're up there tonight, I hope you're listenin' in. Cuz it's called: "I'm Thinkin' of You." Here goes ...

Emily and Annie grab their microphones; Emily sings lead, Annie sings backup. And it's "country" to the hilt.

I'm thinkin' of you every moment,
As though you were here by my side;
I'll always remember the good times,
So darlin' please come back to me.

I'm dreamin' of you every night,
That we were together again;
If time can heal up our partin'
Then love can remove all this pain.

Instrumental - dance break

If love is the secret of livin',
Then give me that love, shinin' light;
When you are again by my side,
Then livin' will once more be right.

75

The audience claps. Emily says, "Thank-you." And then she and Annie join the other women, who have, during the song, loaded themselves, their suitcases, and their lunches into the "van." This van consists of three battered old van seats stuck to the walls of the theater, on either side and up high. The back seat is on the "stage left" side of the theater and the other two are on the other side, the middle seat of the van towards the back of the theater, the front seat, complete with detachable steering wheel, just in front and "stage right" of the stage area. Each seat is lit by its own light.

EMILY:

How much did me and Annie take in singin' at the Anchor Inn?

PELAJIA:

$330 at the door.

MARIE-ADELE:

Solid packed house, eh? Shoulda charged more.

ANNIE:

Fifty bucks for the oom-chi-cha machine. Twenty bucks for Ronnie's guitar. That's our only costs.

EMILY:

Ha! We're laughin'.

A capella reprise of a verse of their song, which fades into highway sounds, and they drive, for a few moments, in silence.

*In the van, driving down the highway to Toronto,
at night. The women have intimate conversations,
one on one, while the rest are asleep or seated at
the other end of the van. Annie is driving. Emily
sits beside her listening to her Walkman, while
Marie-Adele is "leaning" over Annie's shoulder
from her place in the middle seat. Veronique sits
beside Marie-Adele, sleeping. Pelajia and
Philomena are in the very back seat with
Zhaboonigan between them.*

MARIE-ADELE:

Nee, Annie, not so fast.

Pause. Annie slows down.

So. You couldn't get Ellen and Raymond to come along?
I'd like to meet this Raymond someday.

ANNIE:

Angrily insisting on the correct pronunciation.

Raymond! Ellen says he's got a whole library full of
cassette tapes.

MARIE-ADELE:

Annie. You ever think about getting married again?

ANNIE:

Not really. I can hear the band at the Silver Dollar already.

MARIE-ADELE:

Do you still think about ... Eugene?

77

ANNIE:

What're you talkin' about? Of course, I think about him, he's my brother-in-law, ain't he?

MARIE-ADELE:

He made his choice.

ANNIE:

Yeah. He picked you.

MARIE-ADELE:

Annie. I never stole him off you.

ANNIE:

Drop dead. Shit! I forgot to bring that blouse. I mean. In case I sing. Shit.

MARIE-ADELE:

If I'm gone and Eugene if he starts drinkin' again. I see you going for him.

ANNIE:

Why would I bother? I had my chance 20 years ago. Christ!

MARIE-ADELE:

Twenty years ago, I was there.

ANNIE:

Why would I want 14 kids for?

MARIE-ADELE:

That's exactly what I'm scared of. I don't want them kids to be split up. You come near Eugene you start drinking messing things up me not here I come back and don't matter where you are . . .

ANNIE:

I don't want him. I don't want him. I don't want him. I don't want him. I don't want him.

EMILY:

Put us all in the fuckin' ditch!

PELAJIA:

Hey, watch your language up there.

ANNIE:

Shit! I don't care. There's nothing more to say about it. Why don't you take your pills and go to sleep.

Pelajia and Philomena begin talking.

PHILOMENA:

September 8 again.

PELAJIA:

Hmmm? What about September 8?

PHILOMENA:

You don't remember?

PELAJIA:

What?

79

PHILOMENA:
How could you?

PELAJIA:
Mama died?

PHILOMENA:
No! Remember?

PELAJIA:
I can't remember. Got so much on my mind. So many things to forget.

ZHABOONIGAN:
To Philomena.

You like me?

PHILOMENA:
Yes, Zhaboonigan. I like you.

ZHABOONIGAN:
I like the birdies.

PHILOMENA:
You like talking to the birdies?

ZHABOONIGAN:
Yup.

She falls asleep.

PHILOMENA:
Zhaboonigan ... sometimes I wonder ...

PELAJIA:

It's dark ... warm ... quiet ...

PHILOMENA:

Toronto. Had a good job in Toronto. Yeah. Had to give it all up. Yeah. Cuz mama got sick. Philomena Margaret Moosetail. Real live secretary in the garment district. He'd come in and see my boss. Nice man, I thought. That big, red, fish-tail Caddy. Down Queen Street. He liked me. Treated me like a queen. Loved me. Or I thought he did. I don't know. Got pregnant anyway. Blond, blue-eyed, six foot two. And the way he smelled. God! His wife walks in on us.

Long silence.

He left with her.

Long silence.

I don't even know to this day if it was a boy or a girl. I'm getting old. That child would be ... 28 ... 28 years old. September 8. You know what I'm gonna do with that money if I win? I'm gonna find a lawyer. Maybe I can find that child. Maybe I wouldn't even have to let him ... her ... know who I am. I just ... want to see ... who ...

PELAJIA:

I hope you win.

81

Annie and Emily, at the front of the van with Annie driving, are laughing and singing, "I'm a little Indian who loves fry bread." From time to time, they sneak each other a sip of this little bottle of whiskey Annie has hidden away inside her purse.

I'm a little Indian who loves fry bread,
Early in the morning and when I go to bed;
Some folks say I'm crazy in the head,
Cuz I'm a little Indian who loves fry bread.

Now, some folks say I've put on a pound or two,
My jeans don't fit the way they used to do;
But I don't care, let the people talk,
Cuz if I don't get my fry bread, you'll hear me squawk.

ANNIE:

So tell me. What's it like to go to a big bar like ... I mean like ... the Silver Dollar.

EMILY:

Lotta Nishnawbs.[6]

ANNIE:

> *Disappointed.*

Yeah? Is the music good?

EMILY:

Country rock.

---

6 Indians. (Ojibway)

ANNIE:

> *Screams gleefully.*

Yee-haw! Maybe the band will ask me up to sing, eh?
I'll sing something fast.

EMILY:

You would, too.

ANNIE:

> *Sings real fast.*

"Well, it's 40 below and I don't give a fuck, got a heater
in my truck and I'm off to the rodeo. Woof!" Something like that.

EMILY:

Yup. That's pretty fast.

ANNIE:

Hey. Maybe Fritz the Katz will be there. Never know.
Might get laid, too, eh? Remember Room 20 at the
Anchor Inn? Oh, that Fritz! Sure like singin' with him.
Crazy about the way ...

EMILY:

> *Starts singing Patsy Cline's famous "Crazy ...*
> *crazy for feelin' so lonely ..." all the way through*
> *Annie's next speech.*

ANNIE:

... he stands there with his guitar and his 10-gallon hat. Is that what you call them hats? You know the kind you wear kind of off to the side like this? That's what he does. And then he winks at me. *Sings.* "Crazy ..." Oooh, I love, just love the way the lights go woosh woosh in your eyes and kinda' wash all over your body. Me standing there shuffling my feet side to side, dressed real nice and going *Sings.* "Oooh darlin' ..." with my mike in my hand just so. Oh! And the sound of that band behind me. And Fritz. *Sings.* "Crazy, crazy for feelin' so lonely..."

EMILY:

Yeah. You look good on stage.

ANNIE:

Yeah?

EMILY:

How come you're so keen on that guy anyway?

ANNIE:

Sure Veronique St. Pierre isn't just pretending to be asleep back there?

Emily and Marie-Adele check Veronique in the middle seat.

MARIE-ADELE:

Nah. Out like a lamp.

EMILY:

Hey! We'll get her drunk at the Silver Dollar and leave her passed out under some table. Take two beers to do that.

ANNIE:

Hey. Too bad Big Joey had to come back from Toronto before we got there, eh?

EMILY:

Man! That dude's got buns on him like no other buns on the face of God's entire creation. Whooo! Not to mention a dick that's bigger than a goddamn breadbox.

Annie screams gleefully.

How about Fritz? What's his look like?

ANNIE:

After an awkward pause.

He's Jewish, you know.

EMILY:

Laughing raucously.

World's first Jewish country singer!

ANNIE:

Don't laugh. Those Jews make a lot of money, you know.

EMILY:

Not all of them.

ANNIE:

Fritz buys me jeans and things. I'm gonna be one of them Jewish princesses.

EMILY:

What's wrong with being an Indian princess?

ANNIE:

Aw, these white guys. They're nicer to their women. Not like Indian guys. Screw you, drink all your money, and leave you flat on your ass.

EMILY:

Yeah, right. Apple Indian Annie. Red on the outside. White on the inside.

ANNIE:

Emily!

EMILY:

Keep your eye on the road.

ANNIE:

Good ol' highway 69.

EMILY:

Hey. Ever 69 with Fritz?

MARIE-ADELE:

Neee.

ANNIE:

White guys don't make you do things to them. You just lie there and they do it all for you. Ellen's real happy with her Raymond. You can tell the way she sounds on the phone. Maybe someday I'll just take off with a guy like Fritz.

EMILY:

Then what? Never come back to the rez?

> *Annie is cornered. Emily then slaps her playfully on the arm.*

Hey. Know what?

> *Sings.*

When I die, I may not go to heaven,
I don't know if they let Indians in;
If they don't, just let me go to Wasy, lord,
Cuz Wasy is as close as I've been.

ANNIE:

Lots of white people at this Silver Dollar?

EMILY:

Sometimes. Depends.

ANNIE:

How much for beer there?

EMILY:

Same as up here. Nah! Don't need money, Annie Cook. You just gotta know how to handle men. Like me and the Rez Sisters down in Frisco.

ANNIE:

Yeah?

EMILY:

I'll take care of them.

ANNIE:

Maybe we can find a party, eh? Maybe with the band.

EMILY:

Whoa! Slow down, Annie Cook! Easy on the gas!

MARIE-ADELE:

Annie!

Pow. Black-out. They have a flat tire.

The flat tire. Everything now happens in complete darkness.

VERONIQUE:

Bingo!

PHILOMENA:

What was that? What happened?

ANNIE:

I don't know. Something just went "poof"!

EMILY:

Alright. Everybody out. We got a fuckin' flat.

They all climb out of the van.

88

VERONIQUE:
Oh my god! We'll never get to the bingo.

ZHABOONIGAN:
Pee pee.

PELAJIA:
I can't fix a flat tire.

ANNIE:
Emily can.

PELAJIA:
Get the jack. Spare tire.

ANNIE:
Philomena's wearing one.

ZHABOONIGAN:
Pee pee.

PHILOMENA:
This is all your fault, Annie Cook.

MARIE-ADELE:
It's in the back.

ANNIE:
So what do we do?

PELAJIA:
What's the matter with Zha?

PHILOMENA:

Gotta make pee pee.

VERONIQUE:

I knew there was something wrong with this van the moment I set eyes on it. I should have taken the bus.

PHILOMENA:

Oh shut up. Quack, quack, quack.

ANNIE:

Don't look at me. It's not my fault the tires are all bald.

PHILOMENA:

Nobody's blaming you.

ANNIE:

But you just did.

PHILOMENA:

Quack, quack, quack.

VERONIQUE:

Where are we?

ANNIE:

The Lost Channel. This is where you get off.

VERONIQUE:

Groans.

Ohhh!

EMILY:

Yeah, right.

PHILOMENA:

Shhh!

PELAJIA:

Jack's not working too well.

EMILY:

Okay. Everybody. Positions.

VERONIQUE:

Not me. My heart will collapse.

EMILY:

You wanna play bingo?

VERONIQUE:

Groans.

Ohhhh!

ANNIE:

Hurry up! Hurry up!

EMILY:

Okay. One, two, three lift.

Everybody lifts and groans.

PELAJIA:

Put the jack in there.

All lift, except Marie-Adele and Zha, who wander off into the moonlit darkness. Dim light on them.

ZHABOONIGAN:

Ever dark.

MARIE-ADELE:

You'll be fine, Zhaboonigan.

Suddenly, a nighthawk - Nanabush, now in dark feathers - appears, darting in the night.

ZHABOONIGAN:

The birdies!

MARIE-ADELE:

Yes, a birdie.

ZHABOONIGAN:

Black wings!

Marie-Adele begins talking to the bird, almost if she were talking to herself. Quietly, at first, but gradually - as the bird begins attacking her - grow-ing more and more hysterical, until she is shriek-ing, flailing, and thrashing about insanely.

MARIE-ADELE:

Who are you? What do you want? My children? Eugene? No! Oh no! Me? Not yet. Not yet. Give me time. Please. Don't. Please don't. Awus! Get away from me. Eugene! Awus! You fucking bird! Awus! Awus! Awus! Awus! Awus!

And she has a total hysterical breakdown.

Zhaboonigan, at first, attempts to scare the bird off by running and flailing her arms at it. Until the bird knocks her down and she lies there on the ground, watching in helpless astonishment and abject terror. Underneath Marie-Adele's screams, she mumbles to herself, sobbing.

ZHABOONIGAN:

One, two, three, four, five, six, seven ... Nicky Ricky Ben Mark ... eight, nine, ten, eleven, twelve ...

Until the other women come running. Total darkness again.

EMILY:

What the ...

ANNIE:

Marie-Adele!

PELAJIA:

Stop her! Hold her!

VERONIQUE:

What's happening?

PHILOMENA:

Marie Adele. Now, now ... come ... come ...

EMILY:

In the background.

Stop that fucking screaming will ya, Marie-Adele!

PHILOMENA:

Emily. There's no need to talk to her like that now.

PELAJIA:

Help us get her in the van.

PHILOMENA:

Come ... come, Marie-Adele ... everything's fine ...
you'll be fine ... come ... shhh ... shhh ...

> *And they ease Marie-Adele back into the van. Once
> all is beginning to settle down again:*

PELAJIA:

Everything okay now?

PHILOMENA:

Yes. She's fine now.

PELAJIA:

Emily, take over.

VERONIQUE:

Yes. I don't trust that Annie Cook. Not for one minute.

EMILY:

All set?

MARIE-ADELE:

What time is it?

PELAJIA:

Twenty after four.

ANNIE:

Oh! We're over two hours behind schedule. Hurry up. Hurry up.

VERONIQUE:

I'll be exhausted for the bingo tomorrow night. Maybe I should just take 15 cards.

EMILY:

You can rest your heart. And your mouth. All day tomorrow. All set?

> *And she starts up the van. The van lights come back on.*

> *The dialogues resume. Marie-Adele now sits in the front with Emily, who is driving. Zhaboonigan sits between them. Pelajia and Philomena are now in the middle seat, Annie and Veronique in the back.*

EMILY:

You scared the shit out of me out there.

> *Silence.*

Don't do that again.

> *Silence.*

Feeling better now?

> *Silence.*

MARIE-ADELE:

I could be really mad, just raging mad just wanna tear his eyes out with my nails when he walks in the door and my whole body just goes "k-k-k-k" . . . . He doesn't talk, when something goes wrong with him, he doesn't talk, shuts me out, just disappears. Last night he didn't come home. Again, it happened. I couldn't sleep. You feel so ugly. He walks in this morning. Wanted to be alone, he said. The curve of his back, his breath on my neck, "Adele, ki-sa-gee-ee-tin oo-ma,"[7] making love, always in Indian, only. When we still could. I can't even have him inside me anymore. It's still growing there. The cancer. Pelajia, een-pay-seek-see-yan.[8]

PELAJIA:

You know one time, I knew this couple where one of them was dying and the other one was angry at her for dying. And she was mad because he was gonna be there when she wasn't and she had so much left to do. And she'd lie there in bed and tell him to do this and do that and he'd say "Okay, okay." And then he'd go into the kitchen and say to me, "She's so this and she's so that and she's so damned difficult." And I watched all this going on. That house didn't have room for two such angry people. But you know, I said to her, "You gotta have faith in him and you gotta have faith in life. He loves you very much but there's only so much he can do. He's only human." There's only so much Eugene can understand, Marie-Adele. He's only human.

---

7 Adele, I love you. (Cree)
8 Pelajia, I'm scared to death. (Cree)

EMILY:

Fuckin' right. Me and the Rez Sisters, okay? Cruisin'
down the coast highway one night. Hum of the engine
between my thighs. Rose. That's Rosabella Baez, leader
of the pack. We were real close, me and her. She was
always thinkin' real deep. And talkin' about bein' a
woman. An Indian woman. And suicide. And alcohol and
despair and how fuckin' hard it is to be an Indian in this
country. *Marie-Adele shushes her gently.* No goddamn future for them, she'd say. And why, why, why?
Always carryin' on like that. Chris'sakes. She was pretty heavy into the drugs. Guess we all were. We had a
fight. Cruisin' down the coast highway that night. Rose
in the middle. Me and Pussy Commanda off to the side.
Big 18-wheeler come along real fast and me and Pussy
Commanda get out of the way. But not Rose. She stayed
in the middle. Went head-on into that truck like a fly
splat against a windshield. I swear to this day I can still
feel the spray of her blood against my neck. I drove on.
Straight into daylight. Never looked back. Had enough
gas money on me to take me far as Salt Lake City.
Pawned my bike off and bought me a bus ticket back
to Wasy. When I got to Chicago, that's when I got up
the nerve to wash my lover's dried blood from off my
neck. I loved that woman, Marie-Adele, I loved her like
no man's ever loved a woman. But she's gone. I never
wanna go back to San Francisco. No way, man.

MARIE-ADELE:

Comforting the crying Emily.

You should get some rest. Let Annie take over.

EMILY:

I'll be fine. You go to sleep. Wake you up when we get
to Toronto.

Emily puts her Walkman on and starts to sing along quietly to "Blue Kentucky Girl" by Emmylou Harris with its "I swear I love you ..." while Marie-Adele leans her head against the "window" and falls asleep.

After a few moments, Zhaboonigan, who has been dozing off between Emily and Marie-Adele in the front seat, pokes her head up and starts to sing along off-key. Then she starts to play with Emily's hair.

EMILY:

Shrugging Zhaboonigan's hand off.

Don't bug me. My favorite part's comin' up.

Initiated by Zhaboonigan, they start playing "slap." The game escalates to the point where Emily almost bangs Zhaboonigan over the head with her elbow.

EMILY:

Yeah, right. You little retard.

Mad at this, Zhaboonigan hits Emily in the stomach.

Don't hit me there, you little .... Hey, man, like ummm ... I'm sorry, Zha.

ZHABOONIGAN:

Sorry.

EMILY:

Emily feels her belly thoughtfully. After a brief silence:

You gonna have kids someday, Zha?

ZHABOONIGAN:

Ummm . . . buy one.

EMILY:

Holy! Well, kids were alright. Aw geez, Zha, that man treated me real bad. Ever been tied to a bed post with your arms up like this? Whoa!

Grabbing the steering wheel.

Maybe you should drive.

ZHABOONIGAN:

Scary.

EMILY:

Aw, don't be scared. Fuck.

ZHABOONIGAN:

Fuck.

EMILY:

Zhaboonigan Peterson! Your ma'll give me a black eye.

Zhaboonigan turns her head toward the back seat, where Veronique sits sleeping, and says one more time, really loud.

ZHABOONIGAN:

Fuck!

EMILY:

Shhh! Look, Zha. You don't let any man bother you while we're down in T.O. You just stick close to me.

ZHABOONIGAN:

Yup.

EMILY:

We're sisters, right? Gimme five.

They slap hands.

Alright. Bingo!!!

> *Instantly, the house lights come on full blast. The Bingo Master - the most beautiful man in the world - comes running up center aisle, cordless mike in hand, dressed to kill: tails, rhinestones, and all. The entire theater is now the bingo palace. We are in: Toronto!!!!*

BINGO MASTER:

Welcome, ladies and gentlemen, to the biggest bingo the world has ever seen! Yes, ladies and gentlemen, tonight, we have a very, very special treat for you. Tonight, ladies and gentlemen, you will be witness to events of such gargantuan proportions, such cataclysmic ramifications, such masterly and magnificent manifestations that your minds will reel, your eyes will nictitate, and your hearts will palpitate erratically.

Because tonight, ladies and gentlemen, you will see the biggest, yes, ladies and gentlemen, the very biggest prizes ever known to man, woman, beast, or appliance. And the jackpot tonight? The jackpot, ladies and gentlemen, is surely the biggest, the largest, the hugest, and the most monstrous jackpot ever conceived of in the entire history of monstrous jackpots as we know them. $500,000! Yes, ladies and gentlemen, $500,000 can be yours this very night! That's half a million - A HALF MILLION SMACK-EROOS!!! IF you play the game right.

And all you have to do, ladies and gentlemen, is reach into your programs and extract the single bingo card placed therein. Yes, ladies and gentlemen, the single bingo card placed therein, which bingo card will entitle you to one chance at winning the warm-up game for a prize of $20. $20! And all you have to do is poke holes in that single bingo card. Yes, ladies and gentlemen, just poke holes in that single bingo card and bend the numbers backward as the numbers are called. And don't forget the free hole in the middle of the card. Twenty dollars, ladies and gentlemen, that's one line in any direction. That means, of course, ladies and gentlemen, that the first person to form one line, just one straight line in any direction on their card, will be the very lucky winner of the $20 prize. $20! Are you ready, ladies and gentlemen? Are you ready? Then let the game begin! Under the G 56. Etc. . ..

> *The audience plays bingo, with the seven women, who have moved slowly into the audience during the Bingo Master's speech, playing along. Until somebody in the audience shouts, "Bingo!"*

BINGO MASTER:

Hold your cards, ladies and gentlemen, bingo has been called.

The Bingo Master and the assistant stage manager check the numbers and the prize money is paid out.

BINGO MASTER:

And now for the game you've all been waiting for, ladies and gentlemen. Now for the big game. Yes, ladies and gentlemen, get ready for THE BIGGEST BINGO IN THE WORLD ! For the grand jackpot prize of $500,000! Full house, ladies and gentlemen, full house! Are you ready? Are you ready? Then let the game begin!

The house lights go out. And the only lights now are on the bingo balls bouncing around in the bingo machine - an eery, surreal sort of glow - and on the seven women who are now playing bingo with a vengeance on centerstage, behind the Bingo Master, where a long bingo table has magically appeared with Zhaboonigan at the table's center banging a crucifix Veronique has brought along for good luck. The scene is lit so that it looks like "The Last Supper."

The women face the audience. The bingo table is covered with all the necessary accoutrements: bags of potato chips, cans of pop, ashtrays (some of the women are smoking), etc. The Bingo Master calls out number after number - but not the B 14 - with the women improvising responses. These responses - Philomena has 27 cards! - grow more and more raucous: "B 14? Annie Cook? One more number to go! The B 14! Where is that B 14?! Gimme that B 14! Where the fuck is that B 14?!!!" etc. Until the women have all risen from the table and come running downstage, attacking the bingo machine and throwing the Bingo Master out of the way. The women grab the bingo machine with shouts of: "Throw this fucking machine into the lake! It's no damn good!" *etc. And they go running down center aisle with it and out of the theater. Bingo cards are flying like confetti. Total madness and mayhem. The music is going crazy.*

And out of this chaos emerges the calm, silent image of Marie-Adele waltzing romantically in the arms of the Bingo Master. The Bingo Master says "Bingo" into her ear. And the Bingo Master changes, with sudden bird-like movements, into the nighthawk, Nanabush in dark feathers. Marie-Adele meets Nanabush.

During this next speech, the other women, one by one, take their positions around Marie-Adele's porch, some kneeling, some standing. The stage area, by means of "lighting magic," slowly returns to its Wasaychigan Hill appearance.

MARIE-ADELE:

U-wi-nuk u-wa? U-wi-nuk u-wa? Eugene? Neee. U-wi-nuk ma-a oo-ma kee-tha? Ka. Kee-tha i-chi-goo-ma so that's who you are . . . at rest upon the rock . . . the master of the game . . . the game . . . it's me . . . nee-tha . . . come . . . come . . . don't be afraid . . . as-tum . . . come . . . to . . . me . . . ever soft wings . . . beautiful soft . . . soft . . . dark wings . . . here . . . take me . . . as-tum . . . as-tum . . . pee-na-sin . . . wings . . . here . . . take me . . . take . . . me . . . with . . . pee-na-sin . . .

As Nanabush escorts Marie-Adele into the spirit world, Zhaboonigan, uttering a cry, makes a last desperate attempt to go with them. But Emily rushes after and catches her at the very last split second. And the six remaining women begin to sing the Ojibway funeral song. By the beginning of the funeral song, we are back at the Wasaychigan Hill Indian Reserve, at Marie-Adele's grave.

---

9 **Marie-Adele:** Who are you? Who are you? Eugene? Nee. Then who are you really? Oh. It's you, so that's who you are . . . at rest upon the rock . . . the master of the game . . . the game . . . it's me . . . me . . . come . . . come. . . don't be afraid . . . come . . . come . . . to . . . me . . . ever soft wings . . . beautiful soft . . . soft . . . darkwings . . . here . . . take me . . . come . . . come . . . come and get me . . . wings here . . . take me . . . take . . . me . . . with . . . come and get me . . . (Cree)

WOMEN:

Wa-kwing, wa-kwing,
Wa-kwing nin wi-i-ja;
Wa-kwing, wa- kwing,
Wa-kwing nin wi-i-ja.[10]

At Marie-Adele's grave. During Pelajia's speech, the other women continue humming the funeral song until they fade into silence. Pelajia drops a handful of earth on the grave.

PELAJIA:

Well, sister, guess you finally hit the big jackpot. Best bingo game we've ever been to in our lives, huh? You know, life's like that, I figure. When all is said and done. Kinda' silly, innit, this business of living? But. What choice do we have? When some fool of a being goes and puts us Indians plunk down in the middle of this old earth, dishes out this lot we got right now. But. I figure we gotta make the most of it while we're here. You certainly did. And I sure as hell am giving it one good try. For you. For me. For all of us. Promise. Really. See you when that big bird finally comes for me.

Whips out her hammer one more time, holds it up in the air and smiles.

And my hammer.

Back at the store in Wasaychigan Hill. Emily is tearing open a brand-new case of the small cans of Carnation milk, takes two cans out and goes up to Zhaboonigan with them.

10 **Women:** Heaven, heaven, heaven, I'm going there; Heaven, heaven, heaven, I'm going there.   (Ojibway)

EMILY:

See, Zha? The red part up here and the white part down here and the pink flowers in the middle?

ZHABOONIGAN:

Oh.

EMILY:

Carnation milk.

ZHABOONIGAN:

Carnation milk.

EMILY:

And it goes over here where all the other red and white cans are, okay?

ZHABOONIGAN:

Yup.

> *Zhaboonigan rushes to Emily and throws her arms around her affectionately. Emily is embarrassed and struggles to free herself. Just then, Annie enters. She's lost some of her speed and frenetic energy. There's obviously something wrong with her.*

ANNIE:

Hallooo! Whatchyou doing.

EMILY:

Red Lucifer's whiskers! It's Annie Cook.

ANNIE:

Well, we seem to have survived the biggest bingo in the world, eh? Well . . . ummm . . . not all of us . . . not Marie-Adele . . . but she knew she was . . . but we're okay. *Laughs.*   . . . us? . . .

EMILY:

Annie Cook. Sometimes you can be so goddamn ignorant. *Pause.*   Too bad none of us won, eh.

ANNIE:

Philomena Moosemeat won $600. That's something.

EMILY:

Yup. That's one helluva jazzy toilet she's got there, eh?

ANNIE:

She's got eight-ply toilet paper. Dark green. Feels like you're wiping your ass with moss!

EMILY:

Holy!

ANNIE:

I'm singing back-up for Fritz weekends. 25 bucks a gig. That's something, eh?

EMILY:

Katz's whore . . .

ANNIE:

What?

EMILY:

You heard me.

ANNIE:

The Katz's what?

EMILY:

Chris'sakes. Wake up.

ANNIE:

I love him, Emily.

EMILY:

You been drinkin'.

ANNIE:

Please, come with me tonight.

EMILY:

Have to wait for the old buzzard to come pick up this dozy daughter of hers and that's not 'til seven.

ANNIE:

Okay?

EMILY:

Alright. But we're comin' right back to the Rez soon as the gig's over. Hear?

ANNIE:

Thanks. Any mail today?

EMILY:

Sorry.

ANNIE:

That's okay. See you at seven.

And she exits.

ZHABOONIGAN:

Why ... why ... why do you call me that?

EMILY:

Call you what?

ZHABOONIGAN:

Dozy dotter.

> *Awkward silence, broken after awhile by*
> *Zhaboonigan's little giggle.*

EMILY:

Look, Zha. Share a little secret with you, okay?

ZHABOONIGAN:

Yup.

EMILY:

Just you and me, promise?

ZHABOONIGAN:

Yup.

EMILY:

Gazelle Nataways'll see fit to kill . . . but I'm gonna have a baby.

ZHABOONIGAN:

Drops the Carnation milk cans she's been holding all this time and gasps.

Ohhh! Big Joey!

EMILY:

In exasperation.

This business of having babies . . .

And the last we see of them is Zhaboonigan playfully poking Emily in the belly and Emily slapping Zhaboonigan's hand away.

At Eugene Starblanket's house. Veronique St. Pierre is sitting on the steps, glowing with happiness, looking up at the sky as though looking for seagulls. She sees none so she picks up the doll that lies under her chair and cradles it on her lap as though it were a child. At this point, Annie Cook enters.

ANNIE:

Hallooo!

Surprised to see Veronique sitting there.

Veronique St. Pierre. What are you doing here?

VERONIQUE:

Annie Cook. Haven't you heard I'm cooking for Eugene
and the children these days? It's been four days since
the funeral as you know may she rest in peace *Makes
a quick sign of the cross without missing beat.*
but I was the only person on this reserve who was
willing to help with these 14 little orphans.

ANNIE:

That's nice. But I came to see if Simon Star ...

VERONIQUE:

The stove is so good. All four elements work and there
is even a timer for the oven. As I was saying to Black
Lady Halked at the bingo last night, "Now I don't have
to worry about burning the fried potatoes or serving the
roast beef half-raw."

ANNIE:

Well, I was about to ...

VERONIQUE:

Yes, Annie Cook. I bought a roast beef just yesterday.
A great big roast beef. Almost 16 pounds. It's probably
the biggest roast beef that's been seen on this reserve in
recent years. The meat was so heavy that Nicky, Ricky,
Ben, and Mark had to take turns carrying it here for me.
Oh, it was hard and slippery at first, but I finally managed
to wrestle it into my oven. And it's sitting in there at
this very moment just sizzling and bubbling with the
most succulent and delicious juices. And speaking of succulent and delicious juices, did you come to call on
Eugene? Well, Eugene's not home.

ANNIE:

Yeah, right. I came to see if Simon had that new record.

VERONIQUE:

Why?

ANNIE:

I'm singing in Little Current tonight and I gotta practice this one song.

VERONIQUE:

Contemptuously.

That Ritzie Ditzie character.

ANNIE:

It's Fritz the Katz, Veronique St. Pierre. FREDERICK STEPHEN KATZ. He's a very fine musician and a good teacher.

VERONIQUE:

Teacher?! Of what?! As I was saying to Little Girl Manitowabi and her daughter June Bug McLeod at the bingo last night, "You never know about these non-Native bar-room types." I said to them, "We have enough trouble right here on this reserve without having our women come dragging these shady white characters into the picture." Before you know it, you will end up in deep trouble and bring shame and disrespect on the name of Pelajia Patchnose and all your sisters, myself included.

ANNIE:

Myself included, my ass! Veronique St. Pierre. I wish you would shut that great big shitty mouth of yours at least once a year!

VERONIQUE:

Stunned into momentary silence. Then.

Simon Starblanket is not home.

With this, she bangs the doll down viciously.

ANNIE:

Good day, Veronique St. Pierre.

And exits.

Veronique, meanwhile, just sits there in her stunned state, mouth hanging open and looking after the departing Annie.

On Pelajia Patchnose's roof. As at the beginning of the play, Pelajia is alone, nailing shingles on. But no cushion this time.

PELAJIA:

Philomena. Where are those shingles?

PHILOMENA:

From offstage.

Oh, go on. I'll be up in just a minute.

PELAJIA:

Coughs.

The dust today. It's these dirt roads. Dirt roads all over. Even the main street. If I were chief around here, that's the very first thing I would do is . . .

PHILOMENA:

Coming up the ladder with one shingle and the most beautiful pink, lace-embroidered, heart-shaped pillow you'll ever see.

Oh, go on. You'll never be chief.

PELAJIA:

And why not?

PHILOMENA:

Because you're a woman.

PELAJIA:

Bullshit! If that useless old chief of ours was a woman, we'd see a few things get done around here. We'd see our women working, we'd see our men working, we'd see our young people sober on Saturday nights, and we'd see Nanabush dancing up and down the hill on shiny black paved roads.

Annie Cook pops up at the top of the ladder.

ANNIE:

Pelajia for chief! I'd vote for you.

PHILOMENA:

Why, Annie Cook. You just about scared me off the edge of this roof.

PELAJIA:

Someday, we'll have to find you a man who can slow you down. So what do you want this time, Annie Cook?

ANNIE:

Well, to tell you the truth, I came to borrow your record player, Philomena Moosemeat ... I mean, Moosetail. I'm going to practice this one song for tonight. Emily Dictionary is coming to Little Current to watch me sing with the band.

PELAJIA:

It's back from Espanola.

PHILOMENA:

To Pelajia.

Pelajia Rosella Patchnose!

To Annie.

It's still not working very well. There's a certain screeching, squawking noise that comes out of it every time you try to play it.

PELAJIA:

That's okay, Philomena. There's a certain screechy, squawky noise that comes out of Annie Cook every time she opens her mouth to sing anyway.

PHILOMENA:

Yes, Annie Cook. You can borrow it. But only for one night.

ANNIE:

Good. Hey, there's a bingo in Espanola next week and Fire Minklater is driving up in her new car. There might be room.

To Philomena.

Would you like to go?

PELAJIA:
Does a bear shit in the woods?

PHILOMENA:
Glares at Pelajia first.

Yes.

Then quickly to Annie.

Make ... make sure you don't leave me behind.

ANNIE:
I'll make sure. Well. Toodle-oo!

And she pops down the ladder again, happy, now that she's finally got her record player.

PELAJIA:
That Annie Cook. Records and bingo. Bingo and records.

PHILOMENA:
You know, Pelajia, I'd like to see just what this Fritz looks like. Maybe he IS the man who can slow her down, after all.

PELAJIA:
Foolishness! Annie Cook will be walking fast right up until the day she dies and gets buried beside the two of us in that little cemetery beside the church.

PHILOMENA:

Oh, go on.

Pause. As Philomena sits down beside her sister, leaning with her elbow on her heart-shaped pillow.

So, Pelajia Patchnose. Still thinking about packing your bags and shipping off to Toronto?

PELAJIA:

Well ... oh ... sometimes. I'm not so sure I would get along with him if I were to live down there. I mean my son Tom. He was telling me not to play so much bingo.

PHILOMENA:

His upstairs washroom. Mine looks just like it now.

PELAJIA:

Here we go again.

PHILOMENA:

Large shining porcelain tiles in hippity-hoppity squares of black and white ... so clean you can see your own face, like in a mirror, when you lean over to look into them. It looks so nice. The shower curtains have a certain matching blackness and whiteness to them - they're made of a rich, thick plasticky sort of material - and they're see-through in parts. The bathtub is beautiful, too. But the best, the most wonderful, my absolute most favorite part is the toilet bowl itself. First of all, it's elevated, like on a sort of ... pedestal, so that it makes you feel like ... the Queen ... sitting on her royal throne, ruling her Queendom with a firm yet gentle hand. And the bowl itself - white, spirit white - is of such a shape, such an exquisitely soft, perfect oval shape that it makes you want to cry. Oh!!! And it's so comfortable you could just sit on it right up until the day you die!

After a long, languorous pause, Philomena snaps out of her reverie when she realizes that Pelajia, all this time, has been looking at her disbelievingly and then contemptuously. Pelajia cradles her hammer as though she'd like to bang Philomena's head with it. Philomena delicately starts to descend the ladder. The last we see of her is her Kewpie-doll face. And beside it, the heart-shaped pillow, disappearing like a setting sun behind the edge of the roof. Once she's good and gone, Pelajia dismisses her.

PELAJIA:
Oh, go on!

Then she pauses to look wistfully at the view for a moment.

Not many seagulls flying over Eugene Starblanket's house today.

And returns once more to her hammering on the roof as the lights fade into black-out. Split seconds before complete black-out, Nanabush, back once more in his guise as the seagull, "lands" on the roof behind the unaware and unseeing Pelajia Patchnose. He dances to the beat of the hammer, merrily and triumphantly.

END OF PLAY.

118